Politics and Class Analysis

Politics
and Class Analysis

BARRY HINDESS

Basil Blackwell

Copyright © Barry Hindess 1987

First published 1987

Basil Blackwell Ltd
108 Cowley Road, Oxford, OX4 1JF, UK

Basil Blackwell Inc.
432 Park Avenue South, Suite 1503
New York, NY 10016, USA

All rights reserved. Except for the quotation of short passages for the purposes of criticism and review, no part of this publication may be reproduced, stored in a retrieval system, or transmitted, in any form or by means, electronic, mechanical, photocopying, recording or otherwise, without the prior permission of the publisher.

Except in the United States of America, this book is sold subject to the condition that it shall not, by way of trade or otherwise, be lent, re-sold, hired out, or otherwise circulated without the publisher's prior consent in any form of binding or cover other than that in which it is published and without a similar condition including this condition being imposed on the subsequent purchaser.

British Library Cataloguing in Publication Data

Hindess, Barry
Politics and class analysis.
1. Social classes—Political aspects
I. Title
305.5   HT609
ISBN 0-631-15066-8
ISBN 0-631-15067-6 Pbk

Library of Congress Cataloging in Publication Data

Hindess, Barry.
Politics and class analysis.
Bibliography: p.
Includes index.
1. Social classes.   2. Political sociology.
I. Title.
HT609.H56   1987   305.5   87-5208
ISBN 0-631-15066-8
ISBN 0-631-15067-6 (pbk.)

Typeset in 10½ on 13 pt Baskerville
by Joshua Associates Limited, Oxford
Printed in Great Britain by
Billing & Sons Ltd, Worcester

GIFT

Coventry University

Contents

Acknowledgements

I wrote an earlier version of parts of this book for the School of Humanities at Griffith University, and I am grateful to members of the Part-Time Programme for their critical advice and suggestions. Many others have helped in the preparation of this book by discussing some of the issues that it raises and by reading and commenting on draft chapters. I am particularly grateful to Paul Hirst, Ann Jungmann and Elizabeth Kingdom.

1

Introduction

The discussion of class has been one of the major preoccupations of modern social thought for many different reasons (see Calvert, 1982, and Furbank, 1985). Classes have been considered important in relation to politics in one or both of two ways. One is extremely complex and ambitious in its explanatory pretensions: classes are regarded as major social forces that arise out of fundamental structural features of society and they are supposed to have significant and wide-ranging social and political consequences. The other is relatively straightforward, and I will return to it in a moment. My interest in this book is mainly with the first position, and my approach is both expository and highly critical. The aim is to provide a clear account of what is involved in the claims of class analysis and to show why those claims are misleading. Rather than attempt a comprehensive survey of the literature of class analysis, I have concentrated on a relatively small number of representative texts in order to exhibit the structure of their arguments and the unresolved problems within them.

The following two chapters outline the main traditions of analysis that treat classes as social forces and explore some of the differences within and between them. The remainder of the book considers how these traditions have tried to cope with widely acknowledged areas of difficulty for class analysis: the problem of the 'new' middle classes; the position of women in class analysis; and the problems of reductionism. I conclude by arguing that much of the appeal of class analysis rests on an explanatory promise that cannot be fulfilled. The analysis of politics in terms of classes as social forces is at best a kind of allegory, the treatment of a complex subject in the guise of something simple; at worst it is thoroughly misleading.

To see what is at stake in these claims, it may be best to introduce the idea of classes as social forces by way of contrast with the more straightforward approach to the relations between class and politics. Here, the relevance of class to politics is primarily a matter of voting behaviour: class is a feature of social structure that may have some bearing on the political attitudes or values of voters and on the behaviour of political parties. It is in this sense that British election studies have always treated class as one of the major determinants of voting behaviour. For example, the 1983 election study presents the significance of class as follows: 'Broadly speaking, wage-labourers have different interests from those of the self-employed or from those of the salaried managers and professionals. . . . It is the competitive position of different groups in the labour market which provides the basis for differing values and political principles' (Curtice, Heath and Jowell, 1985, p. 14). The claim here is not that class determines political values or voting behaviour, but rather 'that different positions in the division of labour will be fertile soil for distinct social and political values. These values may be inculcated in part by the political parties themselves' (p. 17). The clear implication is that class may be an important influence on political life, as it has been in Britain, or it may not. Other social differences (such as housing tenure, religion, language) may provide 'fertile soil' for distinct values of other kinds, and political parties may inculcate values unrelated to class. Class may be more important in some societies than in others, and its importance may vary over time: it is more important in Britain than in much of Western Europe (Robertson, 1984), and its importance in Britain has declined (Franklin, 1985). Rose and McAllister suggest that, in 1983, 'housing is *the* most important social characteristic influencing voting' (1986, p. 79). On this view, the relevance of class to the understanding of politics in Britain or any other society is a matter for empirical investigation.

Contrast this approach with the idea of classes as major social forces generated by the fundamental structure of capitalist society. In the one case, class is a feature of social structure that may have a more or less significant impact on how people vote, and therefore on the behaviour of parties. In the other, their relation to politics is an intrinsic feature of classes themselves. There are many versions of this position, but it is perhaps most forcefully expressed by Marx and Engels in *The Communist Manifesto*: 'The history of all hitherto existing society is the history of class struggles. ... in a word, oppressor and oppressed, stood in constant opposition to one another, carried on an uninterrrupted, now hidden, now open fight ...' 1968, pp. 35–6). Here the importance of class is not primarily a matter of electoral behaviour. Class position may be closely related to voting behaviour or it may not – but in either case politics is ultimately a matter of class struggle. In Marx's view, classes are the main contending forces in society and they provide the key to the understanding of politics and to the identification of the forces promoting or resisting social change. Class struggle may be overt or it may be hidden, but it is always there.

Now, marxism is by no means the only theoretical tradition to stress the significance of classes as social forces. For an influential non-marxist example, consider the following passage from Goldthorpe's *Social Mobility and Class Structure in Modern Britain*:

The achievement of a genuinely open society would imply, it may be supposed, the decomposition or at all events the serious attenuation of classes in the sense of aggregates of individuals, or families, identifiable in the extent to which they occupy similar locations in the social division of labour over time. However, class structures are ones highly resistant to change: those groupings who enjoy positions of superior advantage and power cannot be expected to yield them up without a struggle, but will rather typically seek to exploit the resources that they can command in order to preserve their superiority. Change is therefore only likely to be brought about through collective action on the part of those in inferior positions, relying on their numbers and above all on solidarity and organization. Hence, an interest in factors influencing their preparedness and capacity for such action – and likewise the strength of resistance on the part of those who are thereby threatened – must follow directly from an attachment to any ideal that is incompatible with a class society. To this extent at least we would agree with Marx: that *if* class society is to be ended – or even radically modified – this can only be through conflict between classes in one form or another. (1980, pp. 28–9)

We will return to Goldthorpe's arguments at several points throughout this book. For the moment notice that although he takes care to distance himself from marxism, Goldthorpe nevertheless insists on the importance of classes and struggles between them for the understanding of social change. Social mobility is important in Goldthorpe's argument precisely because it affects the development of class identification and ties of solidarity, which he regards as necessary for the formation of classes as collective actors.

Goldthorpe's book illustrates one non-marxist approach to class analysis, and I shall refer to several others in subsequent chapters. What the various forms of class analysis share is a common insistence on the importance of classes and the relations between them for the analysis of capitalist societies; they differ in their definitions of class and their accounts of how the idea of class struggle is to be understood. Their common concern with the importance of class analysis and their rather different understandings of what that involves form the principal subject matter of this book.

Following this short introduction are two chapters outlining the main contemporary forms of class analysis. Chapter 2 presents the basic features of marxist class analysis and some of the debates that occur within it. It is organized in three sections. The first introduces some of Marx's programmatic statements of his general approach and takes up an example of his class analysis of

French politics, while the other two sections consider some influential debates within marxism, in part to show that marxism is far from being a monolithic theoretical position. The second section looks at the debates between Lenin and Kautsky around the time of the Russian revolution concerning the class character of parliamentary democracy. The third considers differences between what might be called 'structuralist' and 'sociological' styles of marxist class analysis, taking as an illustration the debate between Poulantzas and Miliband. Despite the striking differences between them, these various positions all exhibit the characteristic promise of class analysis – that the key to the understanding of politics is to be found in class relations and the underlying structures which give rise to them.

Chapter 3 considers the main non-marxist approaches to the analysis of politics in class terms. These positions differ from marxism, and from each other, in their precise definitions of class. They share a common concern with the problem of the emergence of classes as socially significant collectivities out of a system of differentiated class positions. I begin with Weber's discussion in his essay 'Class, status groups, and parties' (1978), and proceed to consider more recent examples of non-marxist class analysis. It is often suggested, especially by marxists, that there is a clear and fundamental distinction between marxist and non-marxist class analysis, and that Weber is the key figure in the non-marxist camp. This chapter concludes with a comparison of marxist and weberian analyses, in order to show that that distinction is not without its problems.

The later chapters consider how class analysis has tried to cope with widely acknowledged areas of difficulty. Two chapters concern the membership of the collectivities, whose struggles are supposed to provide the key to the dynamics of class society. Chapter 4 looks at debates over the 'new' middle classes, that motley collection of more or less well-paid employees who are difficult to classify as capitalists or exploited wage-labourers: managerial and professional employees, teachers, social workers, civil servants and so on. I consider the main marxist and non-marxist manoeuvres employed to conceptualize this group, and show how far it has blurred the distinctions between marxist and weberian class analysis. The second area of difficulty concerns the position of women in the class structure. The traditional approach has been to locate women according to the class position of the 'head' of the household, in most cases that of a husband or father, but this view has been strongly disputed in recent years by feminists and others. Chapter 5 considers the implications of that dispute for the claims of class analysis.

The final widely acknowledged area of difficulty to be considered here is the problem of reductionism, which is discussed in chapter 6. What is at issue is the question of how far politics, law and culture can be understood in terms of classes and the conflicts between them. This is often presented as if it were a distinctive feature of marxist class analysis, but that is misleading in two respects. First, we shall see that the problem also appears in the non-marxist alternatives. In this respect, what is distinctive about marxism is not so much the *existence* of reductionism as a problem, but rather that marxism has always seen it as a problem. Secondly, the reductionism of class analysis takes the form of a gesture rather than a serious programme of work. Marx presents a reductionist project in his Preface to *A Contribution to the Critique of Political economy* and at numerous other points in his work, but it is not systematically followed through; elsewhere he insists on the irreducibility of crucial political phenomena. Marxism has followed his lead in both respects. Reductionism has appeared as a recurrent problem within marxism because of the inconsistency between its insistence on the irreducibility of political life on the one hand and the gestural assertion of a reductionist programme on the other. This point is illustrated by reference to Hobsbawm's commentaries on the British Labour Party's electoral defeats in 1979 and 1983 (Hobsbawm, 1983, 1984, 1985), to an important comparative analysis of the development of social policy in the advanced capitalist societies, and to Przeworski's theoretically sophisticated analysis of socialist and labour movements in Western Europe (Przeworski, 1977). We shall see that similar inconsistencies can be found in non-marxist attempts at the class analysis of politics.

The appeal of class analysis rests on its promise that crucial features of political life are to be understood in terms of relations between conflicting class forces. This usually involves some combination of two elements, both of which I dispute in chapter 7. The first is a notion of classes as collective actors; the second is a conception of the unity and objectivity of the class interests that are pursued by diverse actors in various sites of struggle. I argue that there are indeed actors other than human individuals, but that classes are not among them, and that interests are not objectively given. It follows that the analysis of politics in terms of struggle between classes must be regarded as highly problematic. Classes are not social forces, and the promise of class analysis is one that cannot be fulfilled. To introduce this general argument I return to the comparative analysis of social policy discussed in chapter 6, which claims to relate the development of social policy in the advanced capitalist societies to the balance of class forces in those societies. One implication of this argument is that the working class has more to gain from corporatist arrangements with government and capital than it would lose by agreeing to restrain its industrial militancy. In fact I have considerable sympathy with this general direction of argument. Unfortunately, to the extent that classes and their interests are assigned an explanatory role, the theory is either uninformative or seriously misleading.

However, to avoid possible misunderstandings it is important to be clear what is at stake in my proposition that the appeal of class analysis rests on a promise that cannot be fulfilled. First, it is an argument about class analysis as a general project, rather than some particular marxist or non-marxist version of it. We shall see in chapter 6 that marxist and non-marxist versions of class analysis share a number of problematic features. Secondly, the argument is not that class analysis is unsatisfactory because the world has changed since Marx and others developed their arguments in the nineteenth century. Of course the world has changed in important respects (it would be most disturbing if it had not), but there have been numerous attempts to bring earlier forms of class analysis into line with the changes, some of which I discuss in this book. Thirdly, there is little point in arguing that class analysis is unsatisfactory merely on the grounds that it is incomplete. No serious exponent of class analysis maintains that class analysis tells us all we need to know about the political forces at work in the modern world. The assertion that we must avoid reductionism is commonplace in the literature and everyone now presents some version of Marx and Engels' insistence that other elements must be given their due.

Finally, there is the standard revisionist claim that classes are becoming less relevant. Towards the end of the nineteenth century Bernstein argued that the capitalist economic development had produced a situation in which 'the ideological, and especially the ethical factors [had] greater space for independent activity than was formerly the case' (1961, p. 15). Class, in other words, had been important in the earlier stages of capitalist development but it must now be displaced by a politics organized around the ethical appeal of socialist values. A related argument about the effects of economic growth was advanced in Crosland's *The Future of Socialism* (1956), the most substantial contribution to the 'revisionist' debates of the 1950s in the British Labour Party. Or again, the contemporary literature on 'new' social movements (see the surveys in Cohen, 1983, and 1985) suggests that class struggle has been displaced by other forms of politics in the more advanced societies of the modern world. These are more forceful versions of the claim that class analysis is not so much wrong as it is incomplete. They suggest, in rather different ways, that class analysis has become less informative as non-class forms of politics assume greater importance.

Now there is certainly much that class analysis cannot deal with in the modern world. But in contrast to the various forms of that argument, I make the stronger claim that classes are not social forces at all, and that they never have been. I have suggested that class analysis involves an inconsistent combination of gestural reductionism on the one hand and treatment of crucial political phenomena as irreducible on the other. What is of value in Hobsbawm's discussions of contemporary British politics, or in the other examples of class analysis referred to above, is there in spite of the reference to classes as social forces rather than because of it. Where the idea of politics as class struggle is taken seriously it appears to bring together a wide range of particular conditions and struggles into a unified pattern. In effect, reference to the decisions, interests or other attributes of classes is supposed to perform an explanatory function: for example, where the development of social policy is 'explained' as the product of competing class forces. I argue that the invocation in this way of spurious actors, such as classes, or of objective interests is at best a rather uninformative allegory.

2

Marxist Class Analysis

This chapter presents an outline of the basic features of marxist class analysis and an indication of the range of theoretical and political differences that can occur within it. It is organized in three sections. The first introduces some of Marx's programmatic statements of his general approach and, by way of illustration, looks briefly at an example of his class analysis of French politics. The other two take up some influential debates within marxism to show that marxism is very far from being a monolithic theoretical position. One looks at the debates between Lenin and Kautsky, around the time of the Russian revolution, concerning the class character of parliamentary democracy; the other considers differences between 'structuralist' and 'sociological' styles of marxist class analysis, taking as an illustration the debate between Poulantzas and Miliband.

Marx's theory of history and class struggle

In the social production of their existence, men inevitably enter into definite relations, which are independent of their will, namely relations of production appropriate to a given stage in the development of their material forces of production. The totality of these relations of production constitutes the economic structure of society, the real foundation, on which arises a legal and political superstructure and to which correspond definite forms of social consciousness. The mode of production of material life conditions the general process of social, political and intellectual life. It is not the consciousness of men that determines their existence, but their social existence that determines their consciousness. At a certain stage of development, the material productive forces of society come into conflict with the existing relations of production or – this merely expresses the same thing in legal terms – with the property relations within the framework of which they have operated hitherto. From forms of development of the productive forces these relations turn into their fetters. Then begins an era of social revolution. The changes in the economic foundation lead sooner or later to the transformation of the whole immense superstructure ... (Marx, 1971, p. 21)

Two of the best known shorter excerpts from Marx's work are the passage just quoted from the Preface to *A Contribution to the Critique of Political Economy* and the following two sentences from the first section of *The Communist Manifesto*:

The history of all hitherto existing society is the history of class struggles. Freeman and slave, patrician and plebeian, lord and serf, guild-master and journeyman, in a word, oppressor and oppressed, stood in constant opposition to one another, carried on an uninterrupted, now hidden, now open fight, a fight that each time ended, either in a revolutionary re-constitution of society at large, or in the common ruin of the contending classes. (Marx and Engels, 1968, pp. 35–6)

In other writings Marx and subsequent marxists have provided more sophisticated accounts of various aspects of their approach, but these passages nevertheless give a good concise statement of the most basic features of Marx's theory of history. The Preface gives a schematic outline of the structure of society and the mechanisms of social change, and the passage from *The Communist Manifesto* is a polemical assertion of the role of class struggle in history. I will consider these issues in turn.

In the Preface, Marx presents a model of society as structured by three loosely defined parts or levels, namely, 'the economic foundation', 'a legal and political superstructure' and 'definite forms of social consciousness'. Together these define a mode of production, and its parts are said to be related in such a way that the first plays a primary role, in the sense that changes in the economic foundation of society lead to corresponding changes elsewhere. The economic foundation itself is further divided into 'relations of production' and 'material forces of production'. 'Relations of production' involve definite forms of possession of, or separation from, the means of production. Some examples of different relations of production will be considered in a moment. 'Forces of production' is a loose term referring to forms of organization and integration of distinct labour processes and to various other features that affect the level of productivity of a society. The forces of production of capitalist society would include the complex division of labour, the use of machinery and mechanized transmission within the workplace (as distinct from the limited division of labour characteristic of handicraft production), and the integration of workplaces through market exchanges (as distinct from state planning and other forms of non-market distribution).

The Preface indicates that the relationship between the relations and forces of production provides the general mechanism of social change. Marx suggests that the forces of production have an immanent tendency to develop which inevitably brings them into conflict with existing relations of production (or property relations). This contradiction generates a period of acute social conflict, culminating in the overthrow of the existing relations of production and the formation of a new mode of production. History therefore moves from one mode of production to another, with capitalism representing, in Marx's time, the highest stage of development of the productive forces. Later in the Preface Marx refers to capitalist relations of production as ' the last antagonistic form'. This means that after a period of transition the overthrow of capitalism will lead to a classless society in which productive property is held in common and there are no further contradictions between relations and forces of production.

This model of the structure of society and of historical change may seem straightforward enough at first sight, but it is important to recognize that there are several respects in which it remains obscure. Marx does not clearly define the connections between the three parts of society which he refers to with the words 'on which arises' and 'to which corresponds'. Or again, the assertion that changes in the economic foundation 'lead sooner or later' to transformations elsewhere in society suggests that there may well be periods in which politics, law and 'forms of social thought' do not correspond to the foundation on which they are supposed to arise.

More seriously, perhaps, this general model (of the structure of society and the mechanisms of historical development) is not the product of any systematic demonstration in Marx's work. The Preface states a position, but does not argue for it. In *The German Ideology* (Marx and Engels, 1976) and other works Marx argues strongly for a materialist approach to history, in which material conditions rather than ideas are the starting point of social explanation. There is more than an echo of that position in the Preface. Unfortunately, materialism in that general sense does not explain why the economy rather than, say, politics or kinship and gender relations should be regarded as the 'real foundation on which arises' the rest of society. It is of course trivially true that social life depends on production: those who do not eat do not live to engage in politics. But that truism does not tell us how the economic structure of society is supposed to determine the character of the rest.

In Marx's basic model of society and of societal change the major structural components of society and the relations between them are not rigorously defined, and they are obviously open to a variety of interpretations. This lack of precision in what Marx describes as 'the guiding principle of my studies' is a problem in Marx's theory of history, but it is not a good reason for rejecting it. Theoretical work has to start somewhere, and positions that prove to be inadequate at one stage can always be refined or discarded in later investigations. Marx himself regarded his work as being open to correction. His theories have been the subject of vigorous criticism and equally vigorous defence (for examples, see Cutler et al., 1977, 1978 and Cohen, 1978), and we will consider some of the criticisms below. But few of Marx's most severe critics would deny that his approach has been extraordinarily productive. What should be noted here, however, is an important consequence of Marx's lack of precision. Marxists can agree about the basic model of society and societal change while disagreeing about how exactly it is to be understood, about how precisely law and politics are related to the economic foundation, and how these are related to 'definite forms of social consciousness'. Examples of such disagreements will be considered in later sections of this chapter.

Now, although Marx talks of social revolution in the Preface, he does not refer directly to classes as such or to class struggle. Nevertheless, it is clear from *The Communist Manifesto* and Marx's other writings that class struggle plays a major part in his account of historical change. How do classes fit in to the model of the structure of society sketched in the Preface? That question can be approached from two directions, which indicates a considerable ambiguity in Marx's conceptualization of classes. First, class struggle is the agency of social change: classes are conceived as social forces, as participants in a struggle that takes political and ideological forms. In this sense classes are, or are represented by, political organizations and institutions (political parties, trade unions, state apparatuses) and cultural and ideological forms (for example, by socialist or conservative political doctrines).

Secondly, classes are defined by reference to relations of production. Relations of production involve positions of possession or non-possession of the means of production. Classes consist of those who occupy these positions. In this book we are concerned with classes in capitalist societies, and therefore with capitalist relations of production, but it will be helpful to contrast these with two other kinds of relations of production. Capitalist relations of production define two basic classes: capitalists and workers. Members of the capitalist class possess the means of production in the form of commodities – that is, the land, buildings, machinery and raw materials involved in production are actual or potential objects of commercial transactions. Non-possessors have access to production by means of wage-labour contracts, that is, they sell their labour-power as a commodity. This means that control over production is in the hands of capitalists, since all elements of the production process, including labour-power, are their property. Distribution of the product takes place by means of commodity exchanges between capitalist and capitalist, capitalists and workers (in the exchange of labour-power) and workers and capitalists (in the exchange of consumption goods). Workers are seen as subject to *control* by capitalists and as engaged in *production*. We shall see that this approach leaves considerable room for dispute concerning the class position of employees (i.e. non-possessors) whose job is to control the labour of others and of workers engaged in distribution and financial transactions.

Now consider two other sorts of relations of production. First, in feudal relations of production there are again two basic classes, landowners and serfs. Possession involves the monopoly control of land, and non-possessors have access to land in return for rent (in the form of labour, produce or money). The landowner is therefore in the position of the manager of an estate, controlling both the provision of mills, drainage and other facilities and the use of portions of the land by allocating them to serfs in return for various kinds and levels of rent or by farming them directly with the use of serf labour. Secondly, in petty-commodity production the labourers are also possessors of the means of production, so in this case the relations of production define only one class position. Independent artisans, self-employed professionals and peasants in some societies are engaged in such relations of production.

In Marx's approach to class analysis the forms of possession and non-possession of the means of production have a central place in the identification of classes. Market relations do play an important part in class relations in capitalist societies, but they do so as a consequence of the form in which the means of production are possessed as commodities in capitalist relations of production. Market relations may or may not be present in feudal societies but, on Marx's account, they are not an integral feature of feudal relations of production. We shall see that the market has a very different place in weberian approaches to the identification of classes.

Antagonistic relations of production involve two basic classes, whose different relations to the means of production inevitably create conflicting interests. When Marx refers to bourgeois relations as 'the last antagonistic form', he has in mind the antagonism between the two great classes defined by those relations: the bourgeoisie, who possess the means of production; and the proletariat, who do not. It is the *last* antagonistic form because, in Marx's view, capitalist relations of production will be superseded by possession of the means of production in common. Once that is achieved there is no possibility of antagonism between a class that possesses the means of production and another class that does not.

I will return to some of the problems with this way of identifying classes with particular reference to modern capitalism. For the moment, notice the ambiguity of Marx's discussion of classes. On the one hand, they are defined in terms of opposing positions specified in particular relations of production: bourgeoisie and proletariat, lord and serf, slave-owner and slave, etc. On the other, classes are social forces – in fact the major social forces in history. Why should we identify social forces with the occupants of certain positions in the relations of production? Why should things that are clearly not classes in the latter sense, like political parties, trade unions or newspapers, be treated as if they ultimately represented particular classes and their interests?

These queries reproduce in relation to class the issues raised above in relation to Marx's basic model of society and historical change. In both cases Marx and marxism assume a fundamental relationship between the economy and other features of society – between the 'economic foundation' and other parts of society, and between class in the sense of the occupants of a certain position and class in the sense of a major social force. Just as marxists disagree over the precise interpretation of Marx's model of the structure of society, so they disagree over the precise definition of classes and the connections that are supposed to hold between classes, as defined by relations of production, and the forces engaged in politics and culture. Indeed, different positions on this last issue can be found throughout Marx's own work.

An example of Marx's class analysis: 'The Eighteenth Brumaire'

'The Eighteenth Brumaire of Louis Bonaparte' (Marx, 1968) is an outstanding example of Marx's political analysis. It surveys French political history from the overthrow of Louis-Philippe in 1848 to Louis Bonaparte's *coup d'état* in December 1851. Throughout Europe, 1848 was a year of revolutionary insurrection in the name of constitutional democracy, national self-determination, the abolition of serfdom, and the conversion of all men from subjects of the sovereign into free citizens. With the exception of the emancipation of the serfs in parts of the Austrian empire, the revolution was an almost universal failure. In France, the overthrow of the monarchy in February was followed by crushing defeats for both democratic and revolutionary socialism and then for republicanism. The working class revolt was suppressed, and the victory of the 'party of order' ended in the elevation of Bonaparte to Emperor of France. Marx's discussion of the course of the revolution in France was intended to show that momentous political events could be understood only in terms of their underlying material conditions.

This is not the place for an extended discussion of Marx's classic text, and I use it here simply to introduce two problem areas within marxist class analysis. The first concerns the relations between the economy and the forces engaged in political struggle.

Consider first Marx's comments on what he calls 'the republican faction of the bourgeoisie':

> It was not a faction of the bourgeoisie held together by great common interests and marked off by specific conditions of production. It was a clique of republican-minded bourgeois, writers, lawyers, officers and officials that owed its influence to the personal antipathies of the country against Louis Phillipe, to memories of the old republic, to the republican faith of a number of enthusiasts, above all, however, to French nationalism . . . (Marx, 1968, p. 105)

The two points to notice here are Marx's explicit recognition that this faction is not to be identified by reference to economic conditions, and that the conditions introduced to account for its strength are manifestly non-economic in character. In effect, Marx recognizes the existence of political forces and a field of political conflict that is not immediatly explicable in terms of the effects of economic relations.

So far, so good. Unfortunately his treatment of the two Royalist factions is utterly different, openly disparaging any explanation of their differences in terms of principles and the like:

> what kept the two factions apart was not any so-called principles, it was their material conditions of existence, two different kinds of property . . . That at the same time old memories . . . convictions, articles of faith, and principles bound them to one or the other royal house, who is there to deny this? Upon the different forms of property, upon the social conditions of existence, arises an entire superstructure of distinct and peculiarly formed sentiments, illusions, modes of thought and views of life. (pp. 118–19)

Of course, principles are involved, but only because they are themselves the effects of material conditions, of different forms of property. The difficulty raised by the contrast between these passages is clear. If political conditions are not explicable in terms of material conditions (as the treatment of the republican faction suggests) then 'two different kinds of property' cannot account for what kept the Royalist factions apart. If, on the other hand, political forces are reducible to the effects of material conditions, then Marx has no business treating the republican faction as a real and distinct political force.

What is at issue here is the question of reductionism. It is not a serious problem for the overall argument of 'The Eighteenth Brumaire', but it has been a perpetual source of dispute within marxism. I return to the issue of reductionism in chapter 6, but briefly what is at stake is the question of how far politics, law and culture are explicable in terms of an economic foundation – in terms of classes and the conflicts between them. How far, in other words, does class analysis take us in the understanding of political institutions, ideologies and conflicts? We shall see that the problem of reductionist political analysis is by no means restricted to marxism.

The second problem area to be considered here concerns the tension in the marxist tradition between what might be called 'sociological' and 'structuralist' approaches to class analysis. The first approach operates in terms of a distinction between an objective determination of class position (by reference to relations of production), on the one hand, and a subjective unity of class consciousness, on the other. The point of the distinction can be seen by comparing Marx and Engels's discussion of the proletariat in *The Communist Manifesto* with Marx's comments on the French peasantry in 'The Eighteenth Brumaire'. *The Communist Manifesto* describes the proletariat as developing through various stages, starting with the struggle of individual labourers or of workers in a single factory against their employers, and gradually building up to the class-conscious organization of struggle at a national or even international level by the working class as a whole against the bourgeoisie. At one extreme, the class exists merely as a category of individuals organized, if they are organized at all, into a multitude of local groups. But the growth of capitalist industry leads to a growth in the size of the proletariat, to its concentration in large workplaces and communities and to improved means of communication, which allow for the growth of contacts between different communities of workers. These factors, together with their own experience of struggle against employers and the capitalist state, eventually lead to the integration of the workers into a class-conscious and politically organized collectivity. The proletariat is not a static entity: it is transformed by the dynamics of the capitalist economy, and it transforms itself through the experience of struggle.

Compare that account of the proletariat with the description of the French peasantry in 'The Eighteenth Brumaire':

> The small-holding peasants form a vast mass, the members of which live in similar conditions but without entering into manifold relations with one another. Their mode of production isolates them from one another instead of bringing them into mutual intercourse. . . . In so far as there is merely local interconnection among these small-holding peasants, and the identity of their interests begets no community, no national bond and no political organization among them, they do not form a class. They are consequently incapable of enforcing their class interests in their own name, whether through parliament or through a convention. They cannot represent themselves, they must be represented. (1968, p. 171)

The place of the proletariat in the capitalist organization of production, and the development of capitalism itself, leads in the long run to the class-conscious political organization of the working class as a whole. The character of small-holding peasant production and poor communication between peasant communities effectively rule out the possibility of political organization and collective action by the class as a whole.

What these and other passages suggest is a conceptualization of classes as, first, a category of similarly situated individuals, and secondly, under suitable conditions, as a collective social actor – a cultural and political agency. A class *in itself* is defined by the fact that its members occupy a common position in the organization of production. It becomes a class *for itself* only as a consequence of the members' growing awareness of a community of interests. This awareness would be facilitated by some social conditions and by the experience of collective action, and it would be inhibited by other social conditions. The connection between class as defined by relations of production and class as a social force is made in terms of social conditions leading to collective awareness and the formation of ties of solidarity as the basis of communal action.

Such an account of classes has a clear affinity with the weberian approach considered in the next chapter. Although they define class situation rather differently, both accounts treat it as providing a possible basis for collective action. It is not surprising that many sociologists have been attracted to this version of marxist class analysis, looking for explanations of collective action in terms of awareness of common interests and ties of solidarity.

In sharp contrast to this 'sociological' approach is what might be called the 'structuralist' style of marxist analysis. The term 'structuralism' is used in a variety of different ways in the social sciences. Probably the most common usage refers to a general methodological approach based on features of modern linguistics and widely employed in literary criticism, aesthetic theory and anthropology, especially in France and the USA. In linguistics, 'structuralism' refers to the description and analysis of linguistic features in terms of structures and systems. In its more general usage, 'structuralism' is characterized not simply by a preoccupation with structure, but also with the identification of structures that are supposed to underlie and generate the phenomena under investigation. The best known 'structuralist' in the social sciences is probably the anthropologist Claude Lévi-Strauss. In his analyses of kinship systems and mythology (eg. 1966, 1969), 'structure' refers not to a web of directly observable social relationships, but rather to an underlying reality which constitutes the hidden logic of a social system. 'Structuralism' then is a methodological approach to the analysis of phenomena which refers us to the actions of structures rather than the intentional actions of individuals. Where Lévi-Strauss ultimately refers us to the structures

of the human mind, marxist 'structuralism' refers us to the underlying structure of the social formation. Thus the 'structuralist'
approach to class analysis subordinates the conceptualization of
classes to the basic model of society as a unity of three levels organized around the primacy of the economy. Classes are defined primarily by reference to the economy, but they are represented in
other levels, in politics, law and culture, as a consequence of the
relations of determination between the superstructures and the
economic foundation on which they are supposed to be based.

I will return to the tension between 'sociological' and 'structuralist' class analysis later in this chapter in connection with the
debate between Miliband and Poulantzas. What should be noted
for the moment is that 'structuralist' positions suggest ways of
treating political organizations, ideologies and cultural forms as
representing classes and their interests, even in the absence of class
consciousness and ties of solidarity. The closing sentences of the
passage on the French peasantry quoted above suggest that Marx
regards the peasantry as having a decisive political impact, in spite
of the fact that they are not in a position to form a collectivity or an
organized political force.

The discussion so far has briefly considered Marx's theory of
class and history. It involves a model of society and societal change
and an insistence on the importance of class struggle in history.
That model and that insistence are the common currency of
marxism; it is the acceptance of that currency that identifies a
distinctively marxist approach to class analysis. But I have also
indicated that there are significant ambiguities which allow for
different interpretations of the precise definition of classes and the
relations that are supposed to hold between classes on the one
hand and politics and culture on the other. The common currency
of marxism can be put to radically different theoretical and
political uses. The remaining sections of this chapter take up two
examples of these differences: one a debate over the class character
of parliamentary democracy and the other a dispute between
'sociological' and 'structuralist' approaches to the analysis of the
capitalist state. The aim is not to take sides in these debates, but

rather to clarify what the differences are between the opposed positions and to establish that marxism is far from being a monolithic theoretical or political approach.

The class character of the democratic state

Since their development around the end of the nineteenth century, the representative institutions of mass electoral democracy have posed a problem for marxist class analysis. On the one hand, the democratic state is seen as a capitalist state, that is, as a state serving to reproduce capitalist relations of production and furthering the interests of the capitalist ruling class. On the other hand, the growth of a large and organized working class (the largest section of the population in the more advanced capitalist economies) suggests the possibility of the working class voting its own representatives into power. In effect, class analysis can lead to radically different assessments of the nature of parliamentary regimes. On one side, the democratic state is essentially *capitalist*, indeed in Lenin's view it is 'the best possible shell' for capitalism. On the other side, and precisely because it is democratic, it contains the possibility of a peaceful transfer of state power from the capitalists to the working class.

These opposing interpretations of parliamentary democracy are well represented in a long-running dispute between Kautsky and Lenin in the years before and after the Russian revolutions of 1917. Lenin was a powerful advocate of the 'revolutionary' position, arguing that the capitalist state (democratic or not) must be smashed if the working class is to seize power. This view was opposed by Kautsky well before the Russian revolution, and one of Lenin's best-known books, *The State and Revolution* (1964a), written in 1917, has substantial sections devoted to polemics against Kautsky's brand of socialist politics.

Kautsky was an important figure in the German Social Democratic Party, the largest and best-organized socialist party in the late nineteenth and early twentieth centuries. He worked with

Marx and Engels and was widely regarded as the third leading figure in marxist theory. He was an early advocate of what later became known as the strategy of the 'parliamentary road to socialism', a strategy that has been taken up by most of the western communist parties in the post-war period. Kautsky wrote *The Dictatorship of the Proletariat* (1964) shortly after the Russian revolution. He regarded the Bolshevik seizure of power in 1917 as a betrayal of democracy and therefore of socialism and, since it associated socialism with dictatorship, as a major obstacle to democratic socialist politics in the rest of Europe. Lenin responded with another polemical book, *The Proletarian Revolution and the Renegade Kautsky* (1964b). Although the prestige of Kautsky and the German Social Democratic Party had been damaged by splits over participation in the First World War, Lenin still had good reason to fear the effects of criticism from someone of Kautsky's stature.

The dispute is significant for the present discussion because both Lenin and Kautsky write as convinced marxists, and they make considerable use of the writings of Marx and Engels in support of their arguments. In particular, they both refer to Marx and Engels's comment on the lessons of the Paris Commune in their Preface to the 1872 edition of *The Communist Manifesto*. This suggests that the experience of the Commune, 'where the proletariat for the first time held power for two whole months' makes some details of the *Manifesto* appear dated: 'One thing especially was proved by the Commune, viz., that the working class cannot simply lay hold of the ready made state machinery, and wield it for its own purposes' (Marx and Engels, 1968, p. 99). In Kautsky's view the principal lesson of the Commune is that democracy is an indispensable prerequisite for socialism. The Parisian working class could not simply lay hold of the existing state machine because it was not democratic. They therefore set out to construct a democratic state machine of their own. Lenin counters with the argument that there is democracy and democracy: there is parliamentary democracy, which is an instrument of bourgeois rule, and there is proletarian democracy, democracy for the working class. This dispute raises important issues of democratic theory, some of which I have discussed elsewhere (Hindess, 1983). What matters for present purposes is to see how marxist class analysis can give rise to such radically opposed interpretations of parliamentary democracy.

The validity of a class analysis of politics or of Marx's general model of society is not at issue between Kautsky and Lenin. Rather, it is the question of how precisely politics and the state are to be analysed in class terms. For Kautsky, politics is class struggle: the working class struggles first to obtain democracy, and then uses it to effect the transfer of state power and the socialist transformation of society. Democracy for Kautsky is not just a matter of universal suffrage; it also requires the state machine (the police, the military and the civil bureaucracy) to be subject to parliamentary control, competition between parties for popular support, and freedom of speech and organization. An elected assembly is necessary to secure popular control over central government, and party competition and basic political liberties allow political differences and alliances to be worked out in a relatively open way – they also allow for changes in the party of government. Kautsky therefore insists on the difference between parties and classes: working class power is not to be identified with the rule of a single party claiming to represent the working class.

Kautsky goes on to argue that the capacity of parliament to dominate the state machine varies according to the balance of political forces outside parliament, and especially according to the strength of the organized working class. Where the working class is weak the capacity of parliament to control the activities of the state will be very limited. But, in Kautsky's view, the effects of capitalist economic development will ensure that there is a substantial working class majority in the population. Given universal suffrage, the experience of working class struggle will eventually ensure a parliamentary majority for socialism backed by a powerful and well-organized working class. On this account of the development of politics under capitalism, democracy is the product of popular struggle and once achieved, it provides the institutional conditions in which state power may be held by the bourgeoisie or by the proletariat. Kautsky does not, of course, deny that politics in capitalist democracies is loaded against the left, or that elected parliaments are limited in their capacity to control the state. His argument is that these problems can be overcome by a numerically strong and well-organized working class.

Lenin disputes this possibility. He too sees politics as class struggle, but he also maintains that the institutional conditions of parliamentary democracy provide an arena of political struggle that only appears to be free and open. In fact it is heavily weighted against the interests of the working class. Important sections of the state machine are not within the effective control of parliament; the political freedoms and competition that Kautsky makes such a fuss over in fact work to the benefit of the bourgeoisie through their ownership of the media, control over meeting places, etc. As for the protection of the rights of individuals and political minorities, this is always partial and selective: in practice, in Lenin's view, it favours the parties of the bourgeoisie and the 'democratic' state rarely hesitates to suppress militant organizations of the left. For Lenin democracy is a form of dictatorship by a class: it is always democracy for one class and against another. Parliamentary democracy is democracy for the capitalists and must be overthrown and replaced by popular democracy, the institutional reflection of the interests of the working class and working people generally. On this view, to argue (as Kautsky does) that state power in a democracy may be held by the bourgeoisie or by the proletariat is to ignore the fundamental class determinants of the institutional forms of political life.

A final thing to notice about this dispute is that it is very different in tone from normal academic argument. *The Dictatorship of the Proletariat* is a sustained attack on the Bolsheviks' seizure of state power in 1917 and on their subsequent use of that power. For that reason alone the bitterness of Lenin's response is not surprising. However, there is a more general point to be made here. Lenin and Kautsky were political leaders, not academic social scientists. Indeed, the most influential marxists thinkers – Kautsky, Lenin,

Gramsci, Mao – have all been important political figures, and their major political analyses have been developed in the context of strategic political argument. In that sense marxism has never been just another tradition of academic work – throughout most of its history, theoretical work and social analysis within the marxist tradition have been closely tied to problems of political practice. This link has shown significant signs of weakening over the last 30 years or so as a growing proportion of influential marxists have been in academic positions. Nevertheless disagreements within marxism still frequently carry political overtones that are generally absent from debates within other intellectual traditions in the humanities and social sciences.

'Structuralism' and the human subject

Our second debate concerning the class analysis of the state has a very different character from that between Kautsky and Lenin. It consists of Poulantzas's review of Miliband's book, *The State in Capitalist Society* and a reply by Miliband (both reprinted in Blackburn, 1972). The central issue between them is not so much the class character of the state but rather the methodological question of how it should be analysed. In terms of our earlier discussion of different approaches to marxist class analysis, Poulantzas's argument here is militantly 'structuralist', while Miliband's approach is more nearly sociological in character. Consideration of their arguments will reveal some striking differences regarding the place of the human subject in social analysis.

Poulantzas's argument is organized around two central themes. The first of these is epistemological: it concerns the difference between science and ideology. Briefly, Poulantzas's position is that marxism is a science and that the non-marxist social sciences – economics, sociology, political science – are ideologies. They may be more or less rigorous in their arguments and demonstrations, but they are fundamentally and systematically misleading in their accounts of capitalist society. I have argued elsewhere that such distinctions between marxist 'science' and bourgeois 'ideologies' cannot be sustained (Hindess, 1977), but that argument need not concern us here. It is sufficient to note Poulantzas's view on this point in order to understand his insistence that marxism should have no truck with the 'ideological' concepts of bourgeois social science – for example in his comments on 'elites'. A secondary theme here concerns the alleged effects of theoretical contamination in marxist thought. It leads to theoretical deviations and therefore to political errors, for example, to reformism or a confusion between socialism and trade-unionism.

But it is the second central theme that is important for present purposes. Poulantzas advocates a particularly clear and systematic version of what might be called the 'structuralist' approach to marxist class analysis. I suggested that 'structuralism' provides a way of analysing politics, law or culture in terms of classes and their interests, without assuming class consciousness on the part of the individuals involved. In this loose sense, 'structuralism' is an element in most marxist work: marxist analyses and explanations generally go beyond the consciousnesses of individuals in their discussions of how organizations and ideologies 'represent' the interests of particular classes or fractions of classes.

Marxist 'structuralism' is based on a particular interpretation of the model of society sketched by Marx in the 1859 Preface. It is his elaboration of that model that allows Poulantzas to discuss the position of managers or the role of the state in terms of objective functions rather than in terms of intersubjective relations. Marx refers to the economy as the foundation of the whole super-structure of society. This is what Poulantzas refers to as 'the role of determinant in the last instance': the economic base determines (but only 'in the last instance') the general character of the different parts of society and the relations between them. What these relations are will still vary from one mode of production to another, so that in some cases politics or ideology may play a more important role than the economy in the day-to-day life of the society. That is what Poulantzas calls the dominant role.

On this account, then, we have a complex structure of three levels: an economic base, a political and legal superstructure, and 'forms of social consciousness' (or ideology), interacting with each other in ways that vary from one mode of production to another. Although the economy plays the ultimately determining role, the other levels are nevertheless supposed to have some real effectiveness of their own. That is the point of the qualification, determinant *in the last instance*. What Poulantzas in the first part of his review refers to as 'economism' is the mistake of treating the rest of society as simply reflecting the economic base, forgetting that the other levels are 'relatively autonomous', that is, that they have real effects of their own. Some critics have argued that these notions of 'determination in the last instance' and 'relative autonomy' cannot be coherently sustained. We leave that issue for discussion in chapter 6.

Poulantzas's fundamental argument against Miliband is that a marxist analysis should begin by locating its object within the marxist model of society as a complex structured whole. To neglect that starting point is to allow the ideological concerns of marxism's intellectual opponents to dominate the analysis, and thereby to expose marxism to contamination by bourgeois ideology. For example, in his discussion of Miliband's account of the state bureaucracy, Poulantzas argues that he concedes too much to the opponents of marxism. By concentrating on providing a direct rebuttal of their arguments, Miliband concedes the terms in which they approach the analysis of the state. In effect, he investigates the origins of the leading members of the state machine and tries to demonstrate their social and cultural links with the ruling class.

It is all very well, in Poulantzas's view to collect such information, but it doesn't address the most important question. The relation between the state and the ruling class is an objective relation that arises as a consequence of the structure of capitalist society, not as an effect of the social composition and conduct of the members of the state machine. The latter is really an effect of the structure, not an explanation of it. Poulantzas argues that

Miliband should have established the function of the state within capitalist societies before he investigated the members of the state bureaucracy. Starting from a clear recognition of the function of the state it would then be possible to determine the significance of the social background and other characteristics of the state bureaucracy for the performance of that function. Poulantzas suggests, for example, that it is precisely the fact that the state bureaucracy is not operated directly by capitalists themselves that allows the state to serve the interests of the capitalist class as a whole.

Poulantzas's objection to analysis of the state in terms of the background, values and interpersonal relations of individuals is that it concedes too much to the 'problematic of the subject'. In other words it proceeds as if the human individual were the origin of action, so that explanation has to be grounded in the motivations of individuals. Poulantzas objects that that approach contradicts a principle which he regards as fundamental to marxism, namely, that classes and the state are bearers of objective functions determined by their location in the structure of society. To characterize the class position of managers, for example: 'one need not refer to the motivations of their conduct, but only to their place in production and their relationship to the ownership of the means of production' (Poulantzas, 1972, p. 244). On that view, the action of the structure is the ultimate source of explanation; human individuals are merely its 'bearers'.

I have suggested that marxist analysis always goes beyond the consciousnesses of individuals to locate its analyses and explanations in some discussion of material conditions. Poulantzas' comments on the place of the human subject in marxist theory takes this 'structuralist' tendency to a particularly clear extreme. He dismisses the 'problematic of the subject', in which the individual's will and consciousness appear as the origin of social action, as belonging to the ideological theories of the bourgeois social sciences. He insists that, on the contrary, people are to be treated as bearers of the objective structures and systems of relations in which they are located. The consciousness of individuals cannot explain their actions. They are merely the products of their objective locations and of the part they play in the reproduction of capitalist social relations.

Miliband has little time for such a complete relegation of the individual to an effect of its place in the structure, and he responds by accusing his critic of 'superstructuralism'. Miliband argues that because Poulantzas appears to reduce everything to a matter of objective structures, he ends up with little more than a complicated version of the 'economism' that he condemns in his opening paragraphs. In Miliband's view, the relationship between the state and the various classes is more complex than Poulantzas's 'structural determinism' allows. The values and concerns of managers or of the state elites play an important part in Miliband's account of their behaviour, and he is concerned to investigate the features of their social backgrounds and patterns of social life that sustain those values.

But the supposed effects of the structure nevertheless continue to play an essential part in Miliband's argument. To take just one example, consider what *The State in Capitalist Society* refers to as 'the process of legitimation'. Miliband follows Gramsci in maintaining that the survival of modern capitalist societies depends to a considerable extent on the 'consent' of an overwhelming majority whose real interests lie in the overthrow of capitalism. The real interests of the working class and other oppressed groups are given by their position in the structure of capitalist social relations. In other words, their interests are determined by their position in the structure, and what has to be explained is their failure to recognise those interests and act on them.

The role of consent in this argument follows from the observation that the repressive apparatuses of the state, that is, the police and the military, are not enough to account for the relative political stability of the advanced capitalist societies. The vast majority of the population are very far from a socialist politics committed to the overthrow of capitalism. Yet marxist class analysis tells us that the working class, who form a majority in the advanced capitalist economies, have an objective interest in the overthrow of capitalism, and that they share that interest with other oppressed groups who may not themselves be directly exploited by capitalists. The continued survival of capitalism must therefore be explained by a combination of repression and 'consent'. It is in order to explain that consent that *The State in Capitalist Society* devotes so much attention to what Miliband calls 'the process of legitimation'.

The important points to notice here are first that the problem of consent arises in this form only because Miliband's marxist analysis of capitalism identifies the real interests of the working class and other groups quite independently of any recognition of those interests on the part of the individuals concerned. Miliband disputes Poulantzas's 'superstructuralism' but his own argument is crucially dependent on another structural account of classes and their real interests. Given that account 'the process of legitimation' is brought in to explain why workers (and others) fail to pursue their real interests. It works by inculcating the bulk of the population with ideologies representing the interests of the capitalist ruling class through the actions of a variety of organizations and institutions – churches, political parties, schools, etc. Poulantzas and Miliband disagree over whether these should all be included within the concept of the state, but they agree on their basic function in the maintenance of capitalism.

Secondly, for all the striking differences between them, these arguments of Poulantzas and Miliband clearly exhibit the characteristic promise of class analysis. Different versions of class analysis present their promise in rather different terms, but in all cases it involves the claim that crucial features of the parties, movements, ideologies and other elements of political life can be understood by reference to something more fundamental. My closing chapters argue that this claim is nothing more than a gesture, and that it cannot be substantiated.

3

Weber and Non-marxist Class Analysis

Marxism is far from being alone in its emphasis on class; much non-marxist class analysis has also been concerned with the identification of classes and the relations between them because of their supposed significance as social forces. One of the arguments of this book is that marxist analysis of politics in class terms is not and cannot be successful in its theoretical and political objectives, but it would be a serious mistake to imagine that the alternative accounts of classes as collective actors were any less problematic. If there is a common thread running through the various non-marxist class analyses, it lies in the insistence that no necessary significance attaches to the existence of classes as categories of persons distinguished by their positions in economic relations. This esentially negative point may be developed in two directions, both of which find an inspiration in Weber's work.

The first approach involves a distinction between class and status on the one hand and political organization on the other. A clear implication of Weber's comments on parties in his essay 'Class, status groups and parties' (1978) is that political organization cannot be considered merely an effect or expression of classes or status groups and their interests. Weber's writings on contemporary politics and on modern capitalism generally lay considerable stress on the irreducible significance of bureaucracy, leadership and organization. (See the discussions in Beetham, 1974 and Mommsen, 1974.)

But it is the second direction signalled by Weber that is taken up in non-marxist treatments of classes as collective actors. What matters here is not so much the existence of differentiated class positions, but rather classes as socially significant collectivities. In *The Class Structure of the Advanced Societies*, Giddens identifies a class society as 'one in which class relationships are pre-eminent in the social structure as a whole' (1973, p. 132). But he also insists that there may be considerable 'variation in the specific modes in which class analysis is relevant to the explication of other aspects of the social structure' (p. 134). Very little follows, in other words, from the mere existence of differentiated class positions. A central problem for class analysis therefore concerns the way economic classes become 'social classes' (p. 105). Other authors argue that differential economic locations are far from being the only possible bases for class formation.

Although they may define class positions in different ways, what matters for these sociological alternatives to marxist analyses of classes as social forces is the existence of classes as social realities. This is brought out very clearly in Giddens's discussion. We should not be concerned with the existence or non-existence of classes, in the sense of differentiated sets of economic positions, but rather with their forms of structuration. (p. 20) 'Structuration' here refers to the social processes whereby 'economic' relationships become translated into non-economic social structure. If classes become social realities 'this must be manifest in the formation of common patterns of behaviour and attitude' (p. 111). Or again, 'the existence of class structuration always presupposes at least class awareness, if not class consciousness, and hence implies the existence of differentiated class 'cultures' within a society' (p. 134).

The point, then, is to understand the emergence of classes as 'social realities', to identify first the forms of social differentiation that may provide a basis for class formation and secondly the ties of solidarity and cultural homogeneity that may transform such potential classes into social realities. We begin with Weber's discussion in 'Class, status groups and parties', and then consider more recent examples of non-marxist class analysis.

Class, status and party

In his essay 'Class, status groups and parties' Weber (1978 – or 1968 for a slightly different translation) discusses classes, status groups and parties as distinct but related phenomena of the distribution of power in society. Classes and status groups belong to the economic and social orders respectively, while parties 'are primarily at home in the sphere of power' (p. 55).

To begin with class, notice that Weber defines classes in terms of groupings of related class situations. He uses the term class situation when '(i) a large number of men have in common a specific causal factor influencing their chances in life, insofar as (ii) this factor has to do only with the possession of economic goods and the interests involved in earning a living, and furthermore (iii) in the conditions of the market in commodities or labour' (pp.43– 4). There are several features to notice in this definition. First, class situation is specified in terms of the market situation of the individual. Class situations may be differentiated according to the kinds of property used to obtain returns in some market or, for those without property, according to the types of services offered for sale. Property owners might obtain their income from rent or from commerce. The propertyless may have specialized training or skills that place them in an advantageous market situation and, failing that, they must depend on the sale of their unskilled labour.

The place of the market in this definition of class situation marks an important difference between Weber and Marx. Weber's class situations are phenomena of the commercial life of a society while Marx's classes are phenomena of the organizations of production. Thus feudal relations between landholders and serfs, which do not operate primarily through markets, will be class relations for Marx but not for Weber. Similarly for relations between slave-owners and slaves: Weber notes that slaves are a status group, not a class (p. 45). This difference between Marx and Weber is particularly striking in the case of pre-capitalist societies; it is less significant in the case of modern capitalism, which both conceive in terms of the capitalist organization of formally free wage labour. Both would agree that capitalists and workers occupy different class situations and that the principal source of capitalist profit is the labour of the working class. But even here, Weber's analysis in terms of differential market situations would lead him to find class differences within what Marx would identify as *the* working class.

Notice secondly that in Weber's discussion the existence of common or related class situations does not necessarily define classes as collective actors or as social forces. He does indeed refer to classes and to conflicts between them, but these can only exist where and when there are markets – it is not class struggle that brings markets into being. Weber's definition of class situation in terms of markets means that history cannot be primarily the history of class struggle. Where there are markets, then differential market situations define a variety of distinct economic interests which may or may not provide a basis for collective action.

Weber's discussion brings class situations together into broader classes in two distinct ways. The first is in terms of the character of the market situation involved. Classes may be organized around the ownership and renting of property, especially land and housing, and they may be organized around commercial activity. Within each type we can distinguish those who are positively and negatively privileged, and there may be a number of intermediate positions between the two.

More interesting for our purposes is what Weber refers to as 'social class', defined as 'the totality of those class situations, between which mobility either within the lifetime of an individual or over successive generations is a readily possible and typically observable occurrence' (p. 57). Social mobility is generally defined in terms of significant social boundaries and movement across them, especially between distinct status groups or classes. Restriction of mobility between broadly defined clusters of class situations provides conditions in which similar patterns of life and some conception of common interests might be expected to develop. We shall see that this suggestion is taken up in Giddens's class analysis in which there is a close connection between the patterns of mobility relating (or separating) different class situations, and the existence of classes as 'social realities'. The patterns of mobility and the ways in which it is closed off provide the basis for what Giddens describes as the characteristic three-class system of modern capitalist societies, consisting of upper, middle and working (or lower) classes. In Weber's view, the major social differences in a society may be organized around social classes or around status groups, or some combination of the two. Class predominates in the societies of modern capitalism, and in this respect there are important similarities between weberian and marxist treatments of modern capitalism.

Notice finally that although similar class situations may involve the development of common patterns of life and a conception of common interests there is no necessity for it to do so. Weber insists that 'it is misleading to treat classes as conceptually equivalent to communities' (p. 46). Much of his discussion in 'Class, status groups and parties' is concerned with the conditions in which action in common or organized collective action might emerge from a cluster of related class situations. It depends on cultural conditions of various kinds, on class awareness or more developed forms of class consciousness, and on patterns of social mobility and forms of social closure, which we consider below. This concern with the conditions of emergence of class, as a social collectivity, out of class situations is a recurrent theme of non-marxist class analysis.

Now consider what Weber has to say about status groups. In contrast to classes they are normally communities (p. 48). Status involves an effective claim to social honour or prestige on the basis of some quality or style of life. Status groups are collectivities sharing a common style of life. The common lifestyle and its associated forms of conduct provide the bases for their interaction and for their differential behaviour towards outsiders. Status groups depend on awareness and positive evaluation of those qualities and attributes that distinguish members of the group from others. Status implies a recognition of social differences which 'goes together with a restriction of "social" intercourse' (p. 49). Status is exclusive and it may give rise to an elaborate hierarchy of status differentiations. Weber cites the Indian caste system as an extreme case in which an hereditary division of labour is combined with severe restrictions on social intercourse and especially intermarriage. Status hierarchies develop to the extent that higher status groups successfully operate mechanisms of social closure to keep out those below. Closure mechanisms may involve control over access to specialist training or exclusive forms of education, restriction of interaction to matters of business and impersonal contact, marriage restrictions, and so on.

Weber introduces this notion of social closure in his discussion of status groups, but it has been widely employed by subsequent authors in the context of a distinctively weberian form of class analysis. Weber himself suggests various ways in which class and status differences may be interconnected, especially in relation to the conditions of class action and the formation of social classes. It is clear, for example, that money plays an important part in the maintenance of certain lifestyles, so that membership of status groups may well depend on being in a favourable class situation. Or again, there are cases in which occupational groups use their control over apprenticeship or professional training as a closure device to improve their own market situations. Weber also gives examples of positively privileged property classes acting as status groups in this way. The formation of social classes in Weber's sense presupposes the existence of significant social boundaries which restrict mobility between broad clusters of class situations. The operation of closure mechanisms is one way in which such boundaries are maintained. In effect, classes develop as collectivities to the extent that they take on some of the characteristics of status groups.

Finally, there are parties – the third of Weber's major phenomena of the distribution of power in society. Class and status differences certainly depend on the distribution of power, but Weber insists that parties are 'at home in the sphere of power' (p. 55). A party is any organized grouping concerned to influence the exercise of power. Trade unions, employers' associations, churches, and numerous other groupings may be parties in Weber's sense; they may exist in relation to any locus for the exercise of power, in trade unions or universities as well as in national states. The important thing to notice at this stage is that while parties may represent classes or status groups Weber remarks that they mostly do so 'only in part, and sometimes not at all' (p. 55). This means that, in Weber's view, there are important features of the exercise of power that simply cannot be explained in terms of the interests of classes or status groups.

Class structuration and social closure

The introduction to this chapter suggested that what matters for the sociological alternatives to the marxist treatment of classes as social forces is the problematic character of classes as 'social realities'. We can see what this involves by considering some examples of non-marxist class analysis, beginning with Giddens's *The Class Structure of the Advanced Societies* referred to above. Giddens approaches the question of classes as 'social realities' in terms of the notion of structuration, which refers to the social processes whereby differentiated market capacities become translated into 'classes as identifiable social groupings' (1973, p. 107). Structuration operates at two levels. At the most general, there are factors affecting the overall pattern of connections between the market and the structure of class relations. At this level the most important factor is social mobility: 'Insofar as individuals may move freely within a common cluster of class situations (e.g. a man may move without difficulty from a clerical job in the civil service to one in a business firm) they form a definite "social class"'(p. 16). In effect, Giddens develops Weber's suggestion that the existence of social classes is directly linked to the pattern of opportunities for social mobility in a society. Intergenerational closure is important because it leads to 'the reproduction of common life experience over the generations' while the effect of mobility closure within the career of an individual is to confine movement to 'occupations which generate a similar range of material outcomes' (p. 107). The opportunities for, and restrictions on, mobility associated with the ownership of property, educational qualifications and manual labour-power structure the basic division of modern capitalist societies into three broad classes: 'upper', 'middle' and 'working'.

But within these broad divisions, the specific character of class formation depends on four localized or 'proximate' sources of structuration operating at a localized or 'proximate' level. First, the division of labour between manual and non-manual work involves distinct working conditions, usually in physically separated areas. Secondly, the ownership of productive property gives powers of control over paid employees. Thirdly, the development of bureaucratic systems of authority has given some types of non-manual employees specific powers of control over subordinates; these powers derive from hierarchical systems of administration rather than the ownership of property. Such systems can be found in civil service organizations as well as in private corporations. Finally, there are aspects of modern societies in which status differentiation reinforces class divisions, for example, in patterns of consumption, residential segregation and so on.

These processes of class structuration combine to produce the overall division of society into a small upper class of property owners, a large class of wage labourers and a heterogeneous middle class distinguished by possession of educational qualifications and professional skills. The significance of these divisions may vary but they always involve some level of class awareness and the development of differentiated class cultures. The point of class analysis, then, is to understand the conditions of formation of classes as social realities in a given society, to identify the forms of social structuration that may provide a basis for class formation, and to identify the ties of solidarity and cultural homogeneity that may transform those who occupy a cluster of class situations into a class. Class structuration here is not an all or nothing affair. The existence and significance of class boundaries cannot be settled independently of investigation of the specific forms of structuration at work in a given society. One of the aims of class analysis must therefore be that 'of determining how strongly, in any given case, the "class principle" has become established as a mode of structuration' (p. 110).

Whereas Giddens's discussion is broadly theoretical in character, Goldthorpe's study of social mobility in Britain is of interest as an empirical investigation of social mobility and its consequences for class formation and action. Goldthorpe's concern with mobility is overtly political: the pattern of mobility is important both because it provides a measure of the degree of 'openness' of a society and because it affects the prospects of political action to obtain greater openness. The argument is that a more open society will be achieved only through class struggle; in particular, the working class 'is the social vehicle through whose action, electoral and otherwise, [it has] by far the best probability of being realised' (1980, p. 28).

Social mobility is important then because of its consequences for class formation and the resulting prospects of egalitarian political action. Goldthorpe's study is therefore concerned with the social concomitants of mobility, with the social conditions that foster or inhibit the development of the 'shared beliefs, attitudes and sentiments that are required for concerted class action'(p. 265). Particularly important in this respect are the implications of mobility for the continuity or discontinuity of social relations with 'kin, friends, leisure associates, etc.' (p. 143) and their consequences for cross-class and inter-class ties of sentiment. I return to some of the problems with Goldthorpe's arguments in chapter 5. For the present what should be noted is his insistence that class formation is not simply a matter of the existence of differentiated class situations.

Finally, consider the rather different approaches of Dahrendorf's *Class and Class Conflict in Industrial Society* and Parkin's *Marxism and Class Theory: a bourgeois critique*. Each presents an explicit critique of marxist class theory as a prelude to developing alternative class theories of their own. We are concerned here not so much with the effectiveness of their critiques, but rather to bring out important features of their alternative positions. Dahrendorf develops his structural theory of conflict by means of an analysis of classes as interest groups emerging from structural conditions and effecting structural social changes through their actions (1959, p. ix). The relevant structural conditions, in his view, concern the distribution of authority within imperatively coordinated associations. Classes are dichotomous interest groups defined by exclusion from, or participation in, the exercise of that authority. It is a 'structural' theory of conflict in the sense that the conflicting interests are represented as 'structurally generated orientations' which may be identified independently of the conscious orientations of individuals (p. 173). For Dahrendorf then, as for many versions of marxism, class interests are structurally determined and they may or may not be recognized by the individuals whose interests they represent.

On this account, the emergence of class conflict is not a function of class relations alone, since it also depends on those social conditions necessary for individuals to recognize their structurally determined interests. Dahrendorf offers remarkably little by way of systematic analysis of what those social conditions might be. But he does offer the observation that two kinds of class division appear to be of particular importance in industrial societies: those relating to the exercise of state power on the one hand, and of control within industry on the other. With regard to the latter we are told that the same class interest may be represented in different ways – for example, by competing trades union organizations (p. 181). Dahrendorf has little to say about the social conditions that account for such differentation of the representation of the same structurally determined interest. In effect, then, there is much in Dahrendorf's analysis that parallels the marxism he is at such pains to reject: class interests are determined structurally and quite independently of the consciousness of individuals, and the major agencies of conflict in a society, political parties, trade unions and employers' associations are just so many diverse representations of those structurally determined interests.

Parkin's approach to the identification of classes as socially significant collectivities is different again. Dahrendorf reproduces marxism's problematic disjunction between structurally defined positions on the one hand and the consciousness of individuals on the other. Parkin avoids that set of problems by the simple expedient of not defining classes in 'structural' terms at all, but rather by their mode of collective action (1979, p. 113). Again, whereas Giddens and Goldthorpe concentrate on 'structuration', especially the effects of mobility, Parkin takes Weber's concept of social closure as the central concept in his analysis. Classes are defined in distributional terms as groupings that emerge around structural inequalities, each type of inequality providing a potential for exclusionary or usurpatory forms of collective action. He makes no presumption that any one type of inequality (e.g. those associated with the ownership of productive property) will have effective primacy in a society. The most powerful groups maintain their position by excluding those below them, while those at the other end of the social scale get what they can by means of collective action.

The primary division in society is therefore between the dominant class, who operate primarily through exclusion, and the subordinate class, whose primary strategy is one of usurpation. In effect, privileged groups use their resources to hang on to their goodies, while those at the bottom of the heap must organize in order to use their numerical strength to grab what they can from those above them. Divisions within the dominant and subordinate classes can then be analysed in terms of secondary practices of exclusion and usurpation. In this approach the disjunction between structural position and conscious action disappears because the relevant structural inequalities are themselves regarded as products of collective action by classes or groups within them. But Parkin shares with Dahrendorf – and with marxism – the view that 'classes' are the basic political actors in a society, so that the major agencies of organized conflict and of administration are shown as representing classes and their interests. For example: 'the state can be thought of as a mirror that

reflects the pattern of relations between exclusionary and usurpa-
tionary groups. . . . The nature of the state can, in other words, be
"read-off" from the balance of forces in civil society' (1979, p. 139).

Although Parkin builds on Weber's notion of social closure, his
argument departs from Weber's in two important respects. First,
Weber identifies class positions specifically by reference to
markets, not in terms of social closure. Secondly, Parkin's classes
are identified by their mode of collective action – that is, they are
invariably "communities'. Like Weber's status groups, the existence of Parkin's classes is tied to an awareness of common identity
and to a common mode of action. Nevertheless, his approach is
recognizably 'weberian' rather than marxist – first, because it
depends on an elaboration of some of Weber's arguments (albeit
in a direction not taken by Weber himself); and secondly, because
it analyses class differences in terms of distribution, as affected by
processes of exclusion and usurpation, rather than production.

Marxist and weberian analyses compared

This chapter has proceeded as if there were a clear distinction
betwen marxist and non-marxist class analysis, with Weber as a
key figure in the non-marxist tradition. In fact this distinction is
not without its problems, but our discussion has followed a well
established convention in the literature on class. For example, in
their discussion of the problems posed for most forms of class
analysis by that large collection of employees who do not fit easily
into the categories of capitalist or exploited wage-labourer,
Abercrombie and Urry present weberian and marxist approaches
as the two main traditions, and their survey of the literature is
organized in terms of the distinction between them. It turns out
that Abercrombie and Urry regard that distinction as problematic, and an important part of their argument is directed against
what they call the 'Incompatibility Thesis', namely, that the
marxist and weberian approaches are incompatible. They argue,
on the contrary, that 'any satisfactory theory of class has to solve

problems that are common to both points of view' (Abercrombie and Urry, 1983, p. 11). I return to their arguments in the following chapter. What should be noted here is that marxists and non-marxists often have different views of what is at stake in the distinction between them. On the whole it tends to be marxists who advance the Incompatibility Thesis.

Part of the reason for this difference is a consequence of the way theory and politics are supposed to be related in the marxist tradition. Weber was certainly no socialist, but he did have strong political commitments and there were times when he played an influential part in German politics. Marxists are invariably socialists, however much they may disagree among themselves about the content of their socialism. Commitment to 'weberian' styles of analysis, on the other hand, involves no corresponding political commitment: some who make use of Weber are on the right politically but others are very much on the left. One consequence of this is that while there are certainly ambiguities and inconsistencies in Weber's work, disputes over its interpretation have not had anything like the political ramifications to be found within marxism. Scholars who are recognizably weberian in their overall approach have rarely had the political concern to avoid theoretical contamination, a concern which, as we have seen, is such a prominent feature of much marxist debate.

There has been no weberian political movement to correspond to marxist socialism. In marxist terms there is a clear connection between theoretical and political positions, and it therefore seems important for marxists to defend the integrity of marxist theory against alien intrusions. Lenin's polemics against Kautsky, which were considered in chapter 2, provide a forceful example. He argues that there are clear connections between Kautsky's theoretical deviations and his political stand. Poulantzas too, in his review of Miliband, suggests that there are direct connections between theoretical and political deviations.

Non-marxists on the whole tend to see things rather differently. Even those who have been heavily influenced by Weber rarely identify themselves as 'weberian' in the way that many marxists identify themselves as marxist. Consider the authors discussed in the previous section. There is certainly a sense in which they can be considered 'weberian': Giddens's and Goldthorpe's conception of class in terms of mobility builds on Weber's notion of 'social class'; Parkin takes the concept of social closure (from Weber's discussion of status) as the central concept of his class analysis; and Dahrendorf elaborates a theory of class starting from Weber's notion of imperatively coordinated association. They make use of Weber, but that is not to say that they belong to a political and intellectual 'weberian' tradition on a par with marxism. It is hardly surprising then that non-marxists and marxists often give very different accounts of the relations between the marxist tradition and those forms of class analysis based on Weber. On the one side, we find the view that of course there are differences, but nevertheless Weber's work should be seen as a correction of and supplement to Marx's work, rather than an alternative to it. On the other, we find an insistence on clear and fundamental differences.

The opening chapter of *Economy and Class Structure* by Crompton and Gubbay provides a powerful marxist statement of the Incompatibility Thesis, insisting that the class analyses of Marx and Weber cannot be synthesized. They both define class in relation to the economy, but they do so in radically different ways: whereas Marx locates class in the relations of production, Weber locates them in relation to the market. We have seen that this leads to very different accounts of the class structure of feudal or slave societies, but Crompton and Gubbay also argue that Weber's emphasis on the market generates a partial and misleading account of the class structure of capitalist societies and of their dynamics. In their view, distribution relations are certainly important, but they are themselves a consequence of the relations of production. Weberian analysis in terms of distribution directs attention away from fundamental features of the class character of capitalist society.

It follows that any attempt to combine elements of the marxist and weberian approaches must involve a watering down of marxism's insistence on the primacy of production. For this reason

Crompton and Gubbay describe Giddens as 'neo-weberian' (1977, p. 3), although Giddens represents himself as being extremely sympathetic to marxism. The neo-weberian approach in their opinion, suffers from two major problems. One is that it misrepresents the nature of class conflicts: they are 'not confined to the gaining or losing of market advantage' (p. 3). In marxist terms, working class struggle should be seen as aiming for the overthrow of capitalist society, not just for a redistribution of rewards within it. Secondly, they suggest that important differences in the patterns of distribution between societies do not necessarily entail differences in the underlying class structures.

The fundamental issue at stake here is the way marxism locates class in relation to its account of the dynamics of capitalist society and its more general theory of history. We have seen that Marx's treatment of classes brings together two distinct features. On the one hand, they are defined in terms of opposing positions specified in particular relations of production, and on the other, they are identified as social forces – as the major social forces in history. Two important consequences should be noted here.

First, the class structure of capitalist society is subject to a double dynamic. There is, of course, the dynamic of class struggle itself, but that is compounded by the consequences of capitalist economic dynamics on classes and the relations between them. The development of capitalist economies involves periodic crises and the concentration and centralization of capital, leading to a relative decline in the size of the capitalist class, an increase in the size of the working class, and its concentration into large communities and units of production. We have seen that Marx and Engels's optimistic projections in *The Communist Manifesto* build on some such model of capitalist dynamics. A more elaborated account of the political consequences of capitalist economic dynamics can be found in *The Class Struggle* (1971), Kautsky's commentary on the *Erfurt* Programme of the German Social Democratic Party. More sophisticated accounts of capitalist economic dynamics are available in *Capital* and sometimes in the work of later marxists, but the attempt to draw political conclusions from such accounts is a recurrent feature of marxist analysis.

Secondly, classes exist and have effects whether people recognize them or not. They have conflicting interests and these are exacerbated by the economic dynamics of capitalism. There is, of course a problem about classes developing as self-conscious political actors. Marxists have displayed considerable ingenuity in identifying various processes that interfere with that development to the advantage of the ruling class. But in general, the process of formation of classes as political actors is supposed to be constrained by an objective structure of interests that is already there. To take just one illustration, consider Wright's distinction between class structure and class formation (based on Przeworski, 1977). Where class structure determines what class interests are, class formation 'refers to the formation of organized collectivities within that class structure on the basis of the interests shaped by that class structure. Class formation is a variable. ... If class structure is defined by social relations *between* classes, class formation is defined by social relations *within* classes, social relations which forge collectivities engaged in struggle' (Wright, 1985, p. 10). But why should we treat the formation of organized collectivities as a matter of the formation of *classes*? This question brings us back to Weber.

Weber explicitly repudiated the possibility of constructing a general theory of history. Many commentators have argued that a general theory of history is implicit in Weber's work, and that he has a very clear conception of the nature of modern society and its likely course of development (Beetham, 1974; Mommsen, 1974). Nevertheless, the absence of an explicit model of the essential structure of society and of societal change has important consequences for Weber's discussion of class. Where Marx's account of class forms part of a general theory of history and of the dynamics of capitalist society in particular, Weber's account is more nearly classificatory. There are different types of stratification, and different patterns of class relations, but the question of which predominates in the case of any particular society is a matter of empirical investigation.

For Weber, class struggle may well be important in some situations, but it cannot be the motor of history. Classes exist only where there are markets, so class struggle cannot account for the formation of market relations in the first place, and they provide only one possible basis of collective action amongst others. Thus, even where there are markets, and therefore differentiated class situations, it does not follow that class, rather than status, will be the basis of collective action. There are certainly questions to be asked about the bases of collective action, but they do not take the marxist form of a search for factors that inhibit or encourage the recognition of a structure of 'objective' relations that is always already there. If we take away from marxist class analysis the linkages with Marx's analysis of the economic dynamics of capitalism, then what remains, in terms of Weber's discussion, is a theory of the conditions of class formation that is interesting, but rather limited in scope. It needs to be supplemented by a recognition first, that there may be bases of collective action other than class, and secondly, that there are a variety of ways in which the occupants of class situations may come together to form classes.

4

The Problem of the Middle Classes

The discussion so far has concentrated on presenting the main features of marxist and non-marxist class analysis, and has noted some of the differences within and between these broad categories. The rest of the book will be more concerned with the limitations of what class analysis has to say about modern western societies. Here and in the following chapter, I will consider problems concerning the membership of the collectivities whose struggles are supposed to provide the key to understanding the dynamics of class society. I will then turn to the supposed significance of class analysis for the understanding of politics and consider the class reductionism that appears so often in marxist and much non-marxist class analysis.

Most forms of class analysis identify two basic classes in the advanced capitalist societies, with an intermediate grouping in between, and they do so in terms of broadly economic criteria, relations of production, market situation or property ownership. Even Parkin, who defines classes in terms of strategies of social closure, identifies the two basic classes of advanced capitalist society as a propertied ruling class and a propertyless working class. There are two areas of difficulty within these approaches: one concerns the position of women in the class structure, and this will be discussed in chapter 5; the other is the 'embarrassment of the middle classes' (Wright, 1985, p. 13). Both Marx and Weber recognized the existence of a traditional middle class or petty-bourgeoisie in capitalist society. It consisted of small property owners, independent artisans and professionals, that is, those who lived by the sale of goods or services but were neither employees nor employers of others. Such a group creates no great difficulties for class analysis. The problem of the middle classes arises rather from what is often called the 'new' middle classes, that motley collection of more or less well paid employees who are difficult to classify as either capitalists or exploited wage-labourers: professional and managerial employees, academics, civil servants, and so on. I begin by considering how marxism has dealt with the problem of this group before moving on to discuss weberian analyses. In both cases I concentrate on the various manoeuvres employed in conceptualizing the 'new' middle classes, rather than on their detailed accounts of the class structure.

Marxism and the middle classes

In the 1950s and 1960s it was not uncommon for sociologists to use these new middle classes in support of their arguments that marxism was out of date. For example, in *Class and Class Conflict in Industrial Society*, Dahrendorf argued that marxist class analysis fitted nineteenth-century capitalism reasonably well, but it was unable to cope with the extensive growth of private and public sector bureaucracies. Where marxism stresses possession or non-possession of productive property, Dahrendorf argued that the real divisions in modern societies were between those who exercised authority and those subjected to it. In fact it is not difficult for marxists to respond that the mere size of capitalist enterprises or their ownership by the state does not fundamentally affect their capitalist character. We shall see that marxists have been all too willing to bring authority relations into their accounts of the class structure of modern capitalist societies.

Nevertheless, the enormous growth of the new middle classes during the course of this century has proved an embarrassment for marxist theory. There is no difficulty in finding a class location for the traditional petty-bourgeoisie: they are like capitalists in possessing their own means of production, and unlike them in being dependent on their own labour rather than exploiting the labour of others. Their relations of production are those of what Marx calls petty-production, rather than of capitalist production proper. The situation of the new middle classes is more problematic: they are not in any obvious sense capitalists or exploited wage-labourers, but many do play an important part in capitalist production.

The new middle classes cause difficulties for marxist theory for two reasons. First, although Marx has a great deal to say about different categories of employee in *Capital* and *Theories of Surplus Value* (concerning productive and unproductive labour and the role of management), he does not discuss what bearing the differences between them might have on their respective class positions. Subsequent marxists have tried to remedy that omission and have come up with several ways of dealing with the class positions of members of the new middle classes. The second reason follows from the importance of class in the marxist theory of history – and its analysis of capitalist society in particular. If history is the history of class struggles, and if the role of theory is to provide a guide to political practice, then the task of locating this large and growing section of the population correctly in the class structure has obvious political importance.

In the absence of clear guidance in Marx's writings, marxists have made numerous attempts to conceptualize divisions between working class and non-working class employees. There are several useful discussions of the most important of these attempts (Abercrombie and Urry, 1983; Clegg, Boreham and Dow, 1986; Cottrell, 1984; Wright, 1980). Rather than provide yet another survey of the literature, this chapter adopts a somewhat different approach. We have seen that Marx identifies classes in terms of relations of production, that is, in terms of possession of or separation from the means of production. In the case of capitalism this yields two basic classes: a class of capitalists who possess means of production, and a class of non-possessors, the proletariat. This appears to suggest that the new middle classes are members of the proletariat since they do not possess means of production of their own and are therefore constrained to sell their labour-power to others. Marxists have been reluctant to accept this conclusion in view of the striking divisions within the working class so defined – it is difficult, for example, to think of the executive directors of ICI and their employees on the factory floor as having essentially the same class interests.

Marxists who wish to escape such unpalatable conclusions try to do so in ways that are, as Wright puts it, consistent with 'the general assumptions and framework of marxist class analysis' (1985, p. 26). Two basic moves are available here: one is to identify the working class in terms of exploitation, thereby placing employees who are not exploited in a different class; the other is to locate some employees on the side of the possessors in capitalist relations of production. The most influential marxist conceptualizations of the new middle classes have employed one or both of these manoeuvres. Poulantzas does the latter in his *Classes in Contemporary Capitalism*. The first move is to distinguish those who produce surplus value for capitalists from other employees. This removes workers in the sphere of distribution and circulation from the working class. But this is not sufficient in Poulantzas's view, since the work of managers and technical specialists may also be productive from the point of view of capital. He therefore makes a further move by identifying certain types of employee as performing political or ideological tasks on behalf of capital. In this way classes are represented as having economic, political and ideological determinations. Wright and Carchedi (1977) have tended to argue in terms of the second move, suggesting that elements of the role of capitalist possession may be performed by paid employees and even, in the case of Carchedi, that state employees may be regarded as performing the 'global function of capital'. In his most recent book, Wright relies on a novel version of the first move to argue for the presence of class divisions between capitalist employees in terms of different modes of exploitation. I concentrate here on the two basic moves that underly these various arguments.

Exploitation: productive and unproductive labour

Marx's account of capitalist exploitation is couched in terms of a labour theory of value. An alternative account of exploitation has recently been taken up by some marxists, and I return to its use in class analysis below. In Marx's account workers are employed by capitalists to produce goods and services in return for wages. For all the qualitative differences between them, Marx maintains that the products of labour share the abstract quality of value. They possess value in quantities measured by the labour necessary for their production. Wage levels reflect the value of labour-power, which is given by the value of those goods and services necessary for the reproduction of labour-power, that is, for the maintenance of individual workers and the long term reproduction of the working class as a whole. Marx calls the difference between the value created by the working class and the value of its labour-power 'surplus value'. This is appropriated by the capitalist class as a whole, and distributed amongst them in the form of profit, rent and interest. Capitalist exploitation is the appropriation of surplus value.

Fortunately, neither the details nor the very considerable difficulties of Marx's theory of value need concern us here (but see Cutler et al., 1977, part 1; Steedman, 1981). What should be noted is that any account of economic activity in terms of the creation of value by labour and its appropriation requires that there be some activities which do not themselves create value – for example, the work of capitalists in appropriating their portion of the surplus. Marx calls labour that produces value 'productive', and labour that does not produce value 'unproductive'. Some marxists have tried to use Marx's discussions of the differences between these types of labour as a way of distinguishing between these who belong to the working class (that is, employees who are engaged primarily in productive labour) and those who do not (employees whose labour is unproductive).

Marx makes two basic distinctions. The first concerns labour that is productive or unproductive from the point of view of capital.

Labour expended in the provision of goods or services may be productive from the point of view of those who consume them without necessarily being productive for capital. The issue here is whether the labour is employed by a capitalist in pursuit of profit or is paid for in some other way. For example, furniture may be made by self-employed artisans who live by selling their products to retailers or direct to consumers. Furniture is also produced by capitalist wage-labourers, but in this case the labourers live off their wages, while the capitalist attempts to realize a profit from the sale of what they produce. From the point of view of capital, only this second type of worker is productive. For similar reasons, a servant producing services that are directly consumed by a capitalist rather than sold to a paying customer is not a productive labourer.

Marx's second distinction operates within the ranks of capitalist employees and it depends on the view that certain tasks are essentially unproductive. Surplus value derives from productive labour, but it can be realized by the capitalist only if the product of that labour can be sold. Thus the realization of surplus value by capitalists depends on the performance of other tasks that are not themselves productive of value. To return to our example, the capitalist makes a profit only if the furniture is sold at a suitable price. The work of selling it may be performed by the capitalist or by paid employees, but in neither case is it productive of value. On similar lines Marx identifies various tasks that are necessary to the circulation of goods and services without themselves being productive of value: the labour of buying and selling, book-keeping and the handling and transmission of money.

There is no need to consider the validity of those distinctions here (but see Cutler et al., 1977, chapter 12), but what does concern us is that some marxists have used them to distinguish members of the proletariat, who produce value, from other capitalist employees. For example, Poulantzas maintains that workers in the sphere of circulation and employees of financial enterprises 'simply contribute towards redistributing the mass of surplus-value among the various fractions of capital according to the average rate of profit ... Their remuneration is an unproductive expense ... (1975, p. 212). These workers do not produce value and are therefore not part of the working class. Poulantzas provides an elaborate justification of this position, but he is clearly not alone in treating a large and growing body of wage-earners as if they were not really part of the working class. Railway workers, miners and shop-floor workers in factories are far more likely to figure in socialist conceptions of the working class than are typists, shop assistants and counter-clerks in banks and building societies.

In fact, there is nothing in Marx's discussions of productive and unproductive labour that requires us to interpret the distinction between them as defining two essentially different classes of wage-labourers. Marx's arguments are directed towards the clarification of a conceptual distinction that is required by any labour theory of value, rather than the refinement of his conception of the working class. Poulantzas's notion of a non-proletarian class of capitalist wage-labourers takes off from Marx's discussion, but is certainly not required of it. If we do follow Poulantzas in restricting the working class to the ranks of productive labour as he understands it, then it would be a small minority in the advanced capitalist economies. Wright estimates that it would be no more than 20 per cent in the USA (1980, p. 369). For obvious reasons Wright and many other marxists are not too happy with that result.

There remains a substantial group of employees not yet covered, namely, employees of state agencies and of the numerous quasi-governmental and non-profit-making organizations. They are not productive from the point of view of capital, they do not perform unproductive but necessary labour for individual capitalists and they are not part of the self-employed petty-bourgeoisie. If capitalist class relations encompass owners of productive property and their propertyless employees then we do not have to suppose that all members of society are members of classes. Many marxists would not agree. Again we may take Poulantzas as an example: he argues that the division of society into classes is exhaustive, and that there can be no social groupings external to classes.

In brief, the class struggle and the polarization it involves does not and cannot give rise to groupings alongside of or marginal to classes, groupings without class membership, for the simple reason that this class membership is itself nothing more than the class struggle, and that this struggle exists only by way of the existence of the places of social classes. Strictly speaking, it makes no sense to maintain that there are 'social groupings' that are external to classes but are nevertheless involved in the class struggle. (1975, p.201)

Unfortunately, Poulantzas's conclusion does not follow from the 'simple reason' he gives. Class struggle can exist only if there are classes, but it does not follow that class struggle can exist only if all members of society belong to classes. Poulantzas's view that there can be no significant social groupings outside the class structure is a popular one with marxists. We shall see, for example, that although Wright uses the concept of 'contradictory class locations' to argue that a large proportion of the American population do not have an unambiguous class position, he nevertheless takes care to locate them within a structure of class relations.

Performing the function of capital

The second basic manoeuvre for erecting class divisions within the ranks of capitalist employees is to locate certain categories on the side of possession in capitalist relations of production. This manoeuvre can be made in several ways. Poulantzas constructs one division on the basis of concepts of productive and unproductive labour, but a further division is required in his view because, as we shall see in a moment, Marx regarded much of the labour of management and supervision as productive. Rather than have managers messing up his concept of the working class, Poulantzas uses Marx's discussion of mental and manual labour and of the nature of supervision and management to erect a further division between capitalist employees. Wright (1978, 1980) proceeds rather differently. He suggests that there are three aspects to capitalist control: over the physical means of production, over labour-power and over investment and resource allocation. This allows him to erect a variety of contradictory class locations between bourgeoisie and proletariat and between petty-bourgeoisie and bourgeoisie or proletariat. Carchedi's version is different again. With the notable exception of Clegg, Boreham and Dow (1986) these discussions of the role of managers pay little serious attention to the organizational structure of capitalist enterprises. Once again the details of these attempts need not detain us. What should be noted is that their effect is to remove managerial, professional and various other categories of non-manual employee from the working class on the grounds that they perform political or ideological functions on behalf of individual capitalists or (in the case of senior personnel in the state apparatuses) on behalf of capital as a whole.

Here, for example, is what Marx has to say about the double nature of supervision and management in chapter 23 of *Capital*, vol. 3, 'Interest and profit of enterprise':

> The labour of supervision and management is naturally required wherever the direct process of production assumes the form of a combined social process, and not of the isolated labour of independent producers. However it has a double nature.
>
> On the one hand, all labour in which many individuals cooperate necessarily requires a commanding will to co-ordinate and unify the process, and functions which apply not to partial operations but to the total activity of the workshop, such as that of an orchestra conductor. This is a productive job, which must be performed in every combined mode of production.
>
> On the other hand . . . this supervision work necessarily arises in all modes of production based on the antithesis between the labourer, as the direct producer, and the owner of the means of production. The greater this antagonism, the greater the role played by supervision. Hence it reaches its peak in the slave system. But it is indispensable also in the capitalist mode of production, since the production process

in it is simultaneously a process by which the capitalist consumes labour-power. (1966, pp. 383–4)

Once again, Marx's comments do not necessarily entail a class division between different kinds of employee, but it is not difficult to see how they could be used to argue for such a division. In its second aspect, Poulantzas argues, 'supervision represents part of the *faux frais* of capitalist production' (1975, p. 226). Supervision and management is productive in one respect and unproductive in another. Poulantzas maintains that the work of coordination is never merely technical: it always involves the exercise of power on behalf of capital. Supervision and management therefore reproduce in the workplace 'the political relations between the capitalist class and the working class' (p. 228). Managers are the officers of capitalist production, and for that reason they must be considered petty-bourgeois rather than working class.

> The reason why these agents do not belong to the working class, is that their structural class determination and the place they occupy in the social division of labour are marked by the dominance of the political relations that they maintain over the aspect of productive labour in the division of labour. Their principal function is that of extracting surplus-value – 'collecting' it. They exercise powers that derive from the place of capital . . . (p. 228)

Poulantzas argues for the primacy of the political over the productive aspects of the labour of management, and, therefore, for a political division between management and the working class. Other authors construct class divisions within the ranks of capitalist employees in different ways, but they all claim to derive political conclusions from the class structure they erect. Poulantzas argues that the new petty-bourgeoisie and the traditional petty-bourgeoisie form a single class, on the grounds that they adopt similar political and ideological positions because of their similar relationships to the basic class struggle between bourgeoisie and proletariat (pp. 290–7). Wright's notion of contradictory class locations produces a more differentiated picture: almost half the employed population of the USA are in contradictory class locations, and rather less than a third are in class locations close to the working class. Thus, although there remain significant conflicts of interest, roughly two thirds of the American population turn out to be potential supporters of socialism (Wright, 1980). These various political conclusions all suppose that class analysis has a definite political pay-off. We return to this question in chapter 7.

Notice finally that however this second move is represented, it takes us away from the elegant simplicity of identifying class positions according to possession and non-possession of the means of production. Sections of management may form a specialized and highly paid component of the labour force, but they are employees nevertheless. Poulantzas suggests that the high rewards of senior management are an index of its capitalist character – because they must be paid out of the profits of the enterprise (1975, p. 229). But this argument is entirely circular: it is precisely because he treats managers as capitalists in disguise that Poulantzas can separate their salaries from the labour costs of the enterprise and therefore regard them as profit. Once the straightforward criteria of possession or non-possession of means of production breaks down it is less than clear how marxist treatments of these groups differs from the weberian. I will return to this point.

Another version of exploitation

We have seen that the use of Marx's concept of exploitation to erect a class division within the employed population leaves significant groups of managerial and other non-manual workers in the working class. Marxists who wish to exclude managers, professional employees and the like have therefore turned to the device discussed above. The result, as Wright admits in his latest attempt to conceptualize the class relationships of advanced capitalism, is a 'tendency to substitute domination for exploitation at the core of the concept of class' (1985, p. 56).

Why should that matter? Wright gives two reasons, the first of which concerns the link between class and objective interests. 'The concept of domination does not, in and of itself, imply that the actors have any specific interests . . . Exploitation intrinsically implies a set of opposing material interests (p. 57). The other reason is that analysis in terms of domination gives no particular primacy to class as distinct from other types of domination: 'However, if one wants to retain the traditional centrality Marxism has accorded to the concept of class, then the domination-centred concept of class does pose real problems. (p. 57). In the absence of a prior commitment to the primacy of class and exploitation in political analysis, neither reason can seem particularly compelling.

Fortunately, in Wright's view, a theory of exploitation that does not depend on Marx's problematic value theory has recently been developed by Roemer (1982). Although Roemer's work has not been devoted to resolving the problem of the middle classes, Wright suggests that it can be adapted to that end. Accordingly, in order not to depart from the traditional marxist account of class, he proposes to throw out the traditional marxist account of exploitation and to use Roemer's instead as the basis for his class analysis. We are asked to imagine that the economic life of a society involves various distinct kinds of assets which are controlled to the advantage of some groups and the disadvantage of others. A group is exploited if, first, it would be better off were it to withdraw with its per capita share of the relevant assets, and, secondly, if it is prevented from doing so by the domination of others. For example, the working class suffers capitalist exploitation on this account because it would be better off if it were to withdraw with its per capita share of society's capital assets and it is prevented from doing so by the machinations of the state and other instruments of the capitalist ruling class.

There are three other kinds of exploitation in Roemer's account; feudal, socialist and status. In order to deal with the situation of the middle classes, Wright modifies Roemer's analysis so that we end up with three distinctive kinds of asset relevant to the class analysis of capitalist society: means of production, skills and organization. The first is involved in capitalist exploitation. As for skills, the argument is that most workers would be better off if skills were more equitably distributed. However, it would be difficult to argue that it is domination by the skilled themselves which prevents this. Thus, 'while skills or credentials may be a basis for exploitation, this asset is not really the basis of a class relation (p. 85).

Finally, there are organization assets, which are clearly related to authority and hierarchy.

> The asset is organization. The activity of using that asset is coordinated decision-making over a complex technical division of labour. When that asset is distributed unequally, so that some positions have effective control over much more of the asset than others, then the social relations with respect to that asset take the form of hierarchical authority. Authority, however, is not the asset as such; organization is the asset which is controlled through a hierarchy of authority. (p. 80)

Since the point of adapting Roemer's account of exploitation is to get away from defining the class positions of managers in terms of domination, readers may feel that in this passage Wright protests rather too much.

No matter. If we define groups that are positively and negatively advantaged, and a group in between, for both the skill and organization assets, we end up with a 3 × 3 table of distinct class positions amongst capitalist employees. The effect of analysing advanced capitalist societies in terms of three distinct kinds of exploitation is to identify a considerable variety of class positions. Once again, important political implications are alleged to follow from this analysis. On the assumption that exploitation does indeed generate distinct and opposing interests there are numerous possibilities for class alliances, which Wright explores. He also notes that the overthrow of capitalist exploitation may well leave other forms of exploitation in place.

Weberian approaches

In Weber's view one of the things that distinguishes modern capitalist society from earlier forms of social organization is the ubiquity of the cash nexus: there is no significant economic activity that does not depend on wage-labour and monetary exchange. Everyone lives through the market, and therefore has a market situation and a class position. If the problem for marxism is to find class positions for the large mass of employees who are not readily identifiable as capitalists or as members of the exploited working class, the weberian problem arises from the enormous diversity of middle class occupations.

Throughout this century the advanced capitalist societies have all exhibited a considerable growth of non-manual occupations. There are numerous occupations that could be described as middle class and a large number of people employed in them. They exhibit a wide variety of skills, qualifications and earnings. This raises what Abercrombie and Urry call the 'boundary problem': 'with a class characterized by a great diversity of conditions of its members, it becomes difficult to decide who is a member of the class and who is not' (1983, p. 6). The diversity of conditions means that it is difficult to know where to draw the line between one class and another, and how many lines to draw. Giddens uses the notion of structuration to suggest that there can be no general answer to such questions: 'Class divisions cannot be drawn like lines on a map, and the extent to which class structuration occurs depends upon the interaction of various sets of factors' (1973, p. 273). Nevertheless, while the specific forms of structuration may vary, we have seen that Giddens characterizes the advanced capitalist societies in terms of three broad classes; Parkin identifies two basic classes, and some divisions within each; Goldthorpe, in his study of social mobility in modern Britain, identifies up to seven distinct classes. Another study has the ominous title, from the standpoint of the alleged political significance of class analysis, *The Fragmentary Class Structure* (Roberts et al., 1977).

The 'boundary problem' is most acute in two areas. One concerns the division between working class and middle class. In the late 1950s and 1960s a number of authors argued that the old boundary was breaking down because of the increasing affluence of the working class. Crosland's Fabian pamphlet *Can Labour Win?*, published in response to Labour's electoral defeat in 1959, is one of the clearest examples of this argument (but see also Abrams et al., 1960). Crosland argued that economic growth was leading to a proportionately smaller working class, geographical mobility and the break-up of traditional working class communities. Furthermore, the more prosperous sections of the working class had 'acquired a middle class income and pattern of consumption, and sometimes a middle class psychology' (1960, p. 12). Academic critics had no difficulty in undermining that claim, which they dignified as 'the embourgeoisement thesis'. There was little evidence that affluence had produced the suggested changes in working class political attitudes, and what seem to be the most plausible mechanisms whereby affluent workers might turn into members of the middle class have little empirical foundation (Goldthorpe and Lockwood, 1963; Goldthorpe et al., 1968).

In contrast to the embourgeoisement thesis, a more recent tendency has followed Braverman (1974) in locating the source of change in developments within white-collar occupations. The argument is that the tendency of the capitalist labour process has been to fragment and de-skill the labour force, and that this tendency is not confined to the manual working class. The result has been that certain white-collar occupations involving routine clerical work have become indistinguishable from manual, working class occupations in many respects. The weaknesses of Braverman's arguments have been rehearsed elsewhere (Abercrombie and Urry, 1983; Cutler, 1978). What should be noted here is that while Braverman writes as a marxist, it is far from clear that the processes he claims to describe have any bearing on the *class* position of the workers affected in terms of any of the marxist manoeuvres considered above – except perhaps in terms of

Wright's notion of 'skill' exploitation. To the extent that class is thought to be at stake, as in Abercrombie and Urry's adaptation of the proletarianization argument, it is class in a weberian rather than a marxist sense.

The suggestion that sections of the middle class have now become working class raises the second important aspect of the boundary problem: the location of boundaries within the white-collar world. If some white-collar occupations are now working class, what about the class positions of the rest? Or again, if the enormous diversity of white-collar occupations makes it difficult to identify them as belonging to a single class, must we go to the other extreme and accept that the class structure is 'fragmentary' as Roberts and his associates suggest? The trouble with this conclusion, of course, is that it undermines the political point of class analysis. If the class structure has indeed fragmented then it is difficult to conceive of classes as the basic social forces engaged in promoting or resisting social change. Non-marxist attempts to bring order out of the apparent chaos of white-collar work have been dominated by two fundamental themes: first, the use of both market and work situations to distinguish class positions, and secondly, the concept of a service class.

The suggestion that both market and work situation should enter into the identification of classes was first made in Lockwood's study of office workers, *The Blackcoated Worker*. Market situation refers to 'source and size of income, degree of job security, and opportunity for upward social mobility', while work situation refers to 'the set of social relationships in which the individual is involved at work by virtue of his position in the division of labour' (1958, p. 12).

In effect, Lockwood's suggestion involves two modifications of Weber's definition of class situation in terms of life chances in so far as these are a function of the market. First, he insists that life chances are affected not only by income but also by the availability or otherwise of career opportunities.

Secondly, he treats what happens to people at work as an important feature of their life chances. In this respect, what is particularly significant in Lockwood's argument are opportunities for autonomy and independent decision making on the one hand, and position in a hierarchy of control on the other. In large organizations, of course, independent decision making and control over others tend to go together, and the absence of one often involves the absence of the other. By combining these two criteria it is possible to argue first, that there is an important divide within the white-collar world between those who exercise independent decision making and control and those who do not, and secondly, that opportunities for career mobility mark an important difference between lower white-collar occupations and the working class. On this last point, Abercrombie and Urry argue that the relatively good promotion prospects of the minority of men in clerical occupations exist at the expense of the prospects of the female majority. (1983, pp. 114–8; see also Crompton and Jones, 1984; Heath, 1981, chapter 4). A more general point here is that 'gender itself contributes to the social definition of skill – a minority of jobs are defined as being in the lowest clerical grade not because of the technical content of the work itself, but rather because the job is usually carried out by a woman' (Crompton and Jones, 1984, p. 4). In these respects the work situation of male clerical workers may well be significantly different from that of clerical workers in general.

The second major theme in weberian discussion of white-collar work involves the notion of the 'service class', first introduced by the Austrian marxist Karl Renner (1978). He argues that the expansion of the scale of capitalist enterprises forces the capitalist to employ others to carry out functions that he can no longer perform personally. The capitalist delegates functions to employees, and the capitalist class as a whole delegates functions of control and regulation to employees of the state. These employees are not capitalists: they are a 'service class' because they are employed to perform a service for particular capitalists or for the class as a whole. Renner's service class occupies an intermediate position between the bourgeoisie and the working class. It is identified in terms of the second marxist manoeuvre discussed above.

The term has since been taken up by non-marxist authors and has acquired a rather different connotation. Dahrendorf (1969) locates the service class in the higher reaches of large public and private bureaucracies, thereby identifying them in terms of the exercise of authority, rather than performing services for capitalists. More recently, Goldthorpe has used the term to include 'all higher-grade professionals, self-employed or salaried; higher-grade administrators and officials in central and local government and in public and private enterprises; managers in large industrial establishments; and large proprietors' (1980, p. 39). The last category is anomalous. What the rest have in common is their dependence on the sale of professional or managerial services. In this sense it includes Renner's 'service class'. But by including large proprietors, Goldthorpe removes any suggestion that the service class is an intermediate grouping. His service class is at the top of the hierarchy. Abercrombie and Urry take up a similar position on the grounds that the service class has taken over the performance of the functions of control, planning and conceptualization for capital. However, this take-over has developed alongside the growth of new forms of corporate capital which is often 'depersonalized' in the sense that there are no identifiable human individuals as the capitalists. Such corporate capital is frequently owned by other corporations, insurance companies, pension funds, etc. Consequently, much of the service class serves an impersonal capital rather than individual human capitalists.

Conclusion

The last part of chapter 3 considered what Abercrombie and Urry call the Incompatibility Thesis, that is, the view that marxist and weberian analyses are incompatible. There are indeed differences between them over the precise conceptualization of classes, the analysis of non-capitalist societies and what is particularly distinctive about modern capitalism. Nevertheless at a descriptive level there is considerable agreement about the class structure of modern capitalist societies. In particular, both identify a propertied ruling class, a class of propertyless wage labourers, a class of small property owners and a large propertyless grouping who are neither capitalists nor exploited wage labourers.

This chapter has discussed the problems posed for marxist and weberian class analysis by this last grouping, the 'new' middle classes. The problem for marxism is to identify the class positions of the large number of employees who are neither capitalists nor workers in the traditional sense. Contrary to the claims of some sociological critics, marxism has not been short of conceptual resources for tackling this problem. Those resources have been used to generate a number of different accounts of the class structure of modern capitalist societies. But the result of attempts to conceptualize the positions of the new middle classes has been to weaken the clear cut division between those who possess means of production and those who do not. Discussions based on Marx's account of productive and unproductive labour erect a class division within the ranks of capitalist wage-labourers.

What is at issue in these marxist discussion is an attempt to remove professional, managerial and other well-paid white-collar workers from the working class and to place them somewhere else in the class structure. The bulk of Poulantzas's new pettybourgeoisie and of the occupants of Wright's contradictory class locations combines features of the capitalist possessor with those of the non-possessor. Wright's most recent 'exploitation' approach to class analysis effectively locates their distinctive positions in terms of the possession of special skills and the exercise of authority. Significant political consequences are supposed to turn on the precise conceptualization of these class locations, largely because of the pervasive assumption in marxist thought that there is an intimate connection between class structure and the distribution of objective interests. If we put that assumption to one side, what remains are various ways of dividing up the employed population according to professional expertise, the possession of highly paid skills and the exercise of authority.

The problems of weberian analysis appear to be of a different order. Here it is a matter of how to avoid a fragmentation of the class structure given the enormous multiplicity of middle class occupations and market situations. The point is to bring order into that multiplicity by locating significant social boundaries within it. We have seen that attempts to contain the boundary problem have been dominated by two themes: first, Lockwood's use of both market and work situations to distinguish class positons, and secondly, adaptations of Renner's concept of a service class to describe those who live by the exercise of higher-level professional and managerial skills. Both themes generate a fundamental distinction in the white-collar world between those who exercise independent decision making and control and those who do not.

In effect, then, marxist and weberian attempts to deal with the problems posed by the new middle classes have resulted, as Abercrombie and Urry suggest, in a significant convergence between the two approaches. In particular, they both make use of the distribution of power, knowledge and authority in defining the distinctive class positions of the new middle class.

5

Women and Class Analysis

I have referred at several points to John Goldthorpe's *Social Mobility and Class Structure in Modern Britain*. Goldthorpe's study is concerned with the implications of mobility between classes for class formation and for the prospects of class action to achieve a more open society. Mobility is important in Goldthorpe's view because of its consequences for the social conditions that foster or inhibit the development of the 'shared beliefs, attitudes and sentiments that are required for concerted class action' (1980, p. 263). A large part of the book is therefore devoted to the investigation of 'the wider concomitants of such mobility, as these may be found in *aspects of men's lives* outside the sphere of work – for example, in the accompanying degree of discontinuity in their social relations with kin, leisure associates, etc.' (p. 143, my italics). What of the lives of women? Goldthorpe gives two reasons for restricting the study to the mobility of men. One is apparently technical in character (but see Hindess, 1984): the design of the study required samples of a definite size to be drawn from different age groups, and there were not sufficient resources to provide suitable samples of both men and women. The other reason concerns the limited relevance of women to the British class structure: 'it has been through the role of their male members within the social division of labour that families have been crucially articulated with the class structure and their class fates crucially determined. Or conversely . . . the way in which women have been located in the class structure has reflected their general situation of dependence' (p. 258). With the exception of the minority of women who are '"unattached" or themselves the "heads" of families' (p. 258) the class position of a woman is simply that of her husband or father.

We will return to Goldthorpe's defence of the conventional practice of locating the class position of women by reference to the (presumed male) head of the household. For the moment, notice that the location of women in the class structure raises problems for the major traditions of class analysis of modern Western societies. The discussion so far has effectively treated classes as consisting of individuals whose class positions can be identified in terms of broadly economic criteria, either relations of production or some combination of market and work situation. Chapter 4 examined one area of difficulty for this approach, concerning the position of the 'new' middle classes, that large collection of employees who do not fit easily into the categories of capitalist or exploited wage-labourer.

The position of women in the class structure poses problems of a different order. Modern western societies all contain large numbers of people who are not directly dependent on the market either for paid employment or for income from the ownership of property. This category consists largely of women and children but it also includes several smaller groups such as the institutionalized and the long-term disabled. The most significant questions for class analysis concern the two larger groups, women and children. Class analysis has generally assigned dependent members of the family to the class position of the head of the household. But a large proportion of women are in paid employment in most western societies. Here too, class analysis has assigned them to the class of the head of the household, in most cases that of the husband or father. Thus, whether she is in paid employment or not the class position of a woman is generally decided by the class position of a man. Why are men and women treated differently for the purposes of class analysis? How does class structure relate to the organization of domestic life, to the family or household?

Now, it would be misleading to leave the introduction of the topic of women and class analysis at this point, as if the problems arise simply from the differential treatment of women and men in class analysis. 'Women hold up half the sky' – but what made the situation of women an issue for class analysis was the rise of modern feminism, starting from the late 1960s. Goldthorpe's study appeared in 1980. Had it been published ten years earlier there would have seemed no reason to justify the exclusion of women from the study. Before that time it was simply taken for granted that class analysis was concerned with the positions of men, and by extension with their families. Giddens's *The Class Structure of the Advanced Societies*, first published in 1973, offers little discussion of the class positions of women beyond the following passing comment: 'Given that women still have to await their liberation from the family, it remains the case in the capitalist societies that female workers are largely peripheral to the class system' (1973, p. 288).

The rise of modern feminism has made it impossible to take the 'conventional' view of the class position of women for granted. Feminists have criticized marxism and the non-marxist social scientists for their patriarchal assumptions. Some have suggested an alternative to class analysis based on the centrality of gender relations, and others have argued that gender relations must be regarded as strictly irreducible to those of class. These arguments have raised two interrelated sets of issues for class analysis. One concerns the relationships between class and gender in the analysis of modern societies; the other concerns the location of women within the framework of class analysis, raising questions about the connections between the treatment of class as a matter of individuals (the occupants of certain positions in relations of production or of weberian class siuations) and class structure considered as a structure of families. The following discussion is concerned with the problems posed for class analysis rather than making a contribution to the analysis of gender relations as such.

Class and gender

Many social scientists and many feminists distinguish between sex as a biological category and gender as a social one. The former refers to differences that are biological and the latter to socially constructed attributes associated with those differences. Most societies have a division of labour in child care, and distinctively male and female styles of dress and behaviour. In the modern world, women are far more likely than men to adopt caring and supportive roles in relation to others. What is at stake in the distinction between sex and gender is the claim that patterns of gender relations are not human universals. They may vary from one society to another and within a given society over time and from individual to individual. Some men are better at caring for others than most women, and some women are worse at it than most men.

The socially constructed character of gender relations is a matter of some dispute. Sociobiology has tended to argue that the underlying structure of relations between men and women is vested in biological differences that are the product of human evolution (for example Wilson, 1975, 1978). Radical feminists have sometimes adopted a similar position. One of the clearest examples is the American feminist Firestone: 'The sexual reproductive organization of society always furnishes the real basis, starting from which we can alone work out the ultimate explanation of the whole superstructure of economic, juridical and political institutions as well as the religious, philosophical and other ideas of a given historical period' (1972, p. 21). The parallel with Marx's schematic account of his basic theory of history in the 1859 Preface is clear (e.g. in the notions of real basis and superstructure) and intended. Firestone uses the term 'sex class' and her objective is to substitute sex for class in a materialist account of history. Oppressive relations between men and women are biologically determined, and they can be overcome only by revolutionizing the process of reproduction itself.

Now, the reason so many feminists and social scientists insist on the distinction between sex and gender is precisely in order to be able to dispute the biological determinism of such positions. Barrett argues that they are reductionist in that they subsume complex, socially and historically constructed phenomena under the simple category of biological difference. 'Furthermore, the political and ideological role of such arguments is inevitably reactionary, since if particular social arrangements are held to be "naturally" given, there is little we can do to change them' (1980, p. 13). Quite so – but we should be wary of the implied suggestion that we can always do something to change social arrangements that are not naturally given. To say that certain features of social arrangements may vary from society to society is not necessarily to say that they are readily amenable to deliberate political action.

However, the important point to notice here is that questions of the relations between class, on the one hand, and relations between men and women, on the other, raises issues of far-reaching theoretical and political significance – at least from the point of view of those who see class analysis as the key to the understanding of modern society. Barrett presents the issue for marxist class analysis in the following terms:

> [Marxism] is grounded in concepts that do not and could not address directly the gender of the exploiters and those whose labour is appropriated. A marxist analysis of capitalism is therefore conceived around a primary contradiction between labour and capital and operates with categories that . . . can be termed 'sex-blind'. Feminism, however, points in a different direction, emphasising precisely the relations of gender – largely speaking, of the oppression of women by men – that marxism has tended to pass over in silence. (p. 8)

The problem for marxist feminists, she argues, is how to reconcile an approach to social analysis based on the primacy of relations of production with a feminist insistence on the importance and specific character of gender relations.

In fact, of course, the feminist emphasis on gender relations does nothing to establish their analytical independence. Marxism has been far from silent about the oppression of women, which it has tried to explain as a specific product of capitalism or of class relations generally. The implication is that the oppression of women can be ended only with the overthrow of capitalism and the establishment of a classless society. Feminist political objectives are therefore best pursued through support of socialist class struggle. To show that gender relations must be considered (by marxists) as irreducible to class, it is necessary to demonstate that marxist accounts of the oppression of women are unsatisfactory – and Barrett's first chapter surveys the theories that have been advanced on this score. Since the argument of this book is that class analysis does not provide the key to understanding modern (or any other) society, there is no need to consider these specific discussions here.

Barrett takes what might be called a minimalist position on the relations between class and gender: gender is distinct from and irreducible to class, but the precise relationships between them remain to be established. Others have gone further, arguing that gender rather than class should be accorded primacy in social analysis (Firestone (1972)), or that class and gender relations are two analytically distinct systems. As an example of the latter, Delphy maintains 'that patriarchy is the system of subordination of women to men in contemporary industiral societies, that this system has an economic base, and that this base is the domestic mode of production' (1984. p. 18). From this point of view patriarchal 'class' relations between women and men cut across the system of capitalist class relations. Stratification studies make use of their dependent status within patriarchal relations in order to put women in the same social class as their husbands. In Delphy's view, this practice of assigning husband and wife to the same social class obscures the exploitative relationship between them: 'it is about as accurate to say that the wife of a bourgeois man is herself bourgeois as it is to say that the slave of a plantation owner is himself a plantation owner' (p. 72).

The differences between these various positions need not concern us here. What should be noted is that they all pose severe problems for marxist class analysis, or indeed for any other position that sees class as the key to the understanding of modern society. Barrett's plaintive comment on Delphy's argument makes the point very clearly: 'The difficulty here is that the category of patriarchy is assigned analytical independence vis-a-vis the capitalist mode of production, but we are not led to a systematic consideration of the relations between them' (1980, p. 14). In other words, Delphy's account of patriarchal 'class' relations is not integrated into the traditional marxist account of capitalism. The reason for that lack of integration is not difficult to see. The theory of patriarchy offers one explanatory principle and the marxist analysis of capitalism offers another. To bring them together would be to combine the primacy of capitalist relations of production with the irreducibility and autonomy of patriarchy. The combination is incoherent (Adlam, 1979, Cousins, 1978). Barrett's tortuous discussion of the problems of marxist feminism exemplifies the consequences of refusing to accept that conclusion. This problem for marxism is one instance of a more general confusion over reductionism which is discused in chapter 6.

Notice, finally, a further issue that arises from the treatment of gender as defining distinct and opposed social categories on a par with classes. Leaving questions of coherence to one side, the result of adding a theory of patriarchy to marxist class analysis is to introduce a further division of objective interests within capitalist society. Depending on how the various 'interests' are thought to line up, this makes it possible to maintain, with Delphy, that men are the main enemy of women, that the working class and women share a common interest in socialism (for example Hobsbawm, 1983, 1984, 1985, and the various editions of the programme of the British Communist Party, *The British Road to Socialism*), or that trade union commitment to the family wage principle involves a collusion between capital and the male working class (e.g. Barrett and McIntosh, 1980). What is at stake in these positions is the idea that political analysis can proceed on the basis of a conception of interests as given by features of individuals social location, quite independently of whether the individuals' in question recognize those interests as their own or not. We return to the problems with that idea in chapter 7.

The location of women in the class structure

The introduction to this chapter referred to Goldthorpe's defence of the practice of identifying the class position of women by reference to that of the head of the household. For most women this means that their class position is that of their husband or father. A minority may live independently or themselves be the heads of households, in which case their class position is determined by their own position in capitalist economic relations. In general, however, the conventional view involves a differential treatment of men and women. The class position of men is given by their own occupational situation, while the class position of women is that of someone else.

In effect, this conventional view involves two fundamental assumptions: first, that the class structure is a structure of conjugal families, not of individuals, and secondly, that the class position of the family is given by that of the head of the family in the occupational structure. In Goldthorpe's view it is the family head 'who has the fullest commitment to participation in the labour market' and who has 'what might be termed a directly determined position within the class structure' (1983, p. 468). If labour-market participation is the crucial consideration here, then, of course, it is possible that the position of the wife rather than that of the husband 'determines the family class position' (1984c, p. 498). But in most cases the class position of the family is given by that of a man. The derivative class position of women therefore reflects their generally subordinate position within the family.

The conventional view has been the subject of considerable dispute in recent years. Goldthorpe offered a further defence in *Sociology* (1983), which sparked off another round of debate in subsequent issues of that journal. Critics have argued that the assumptions of the conventional view accurately reflect the true position of women in our societies (Delphy, 1984); that class analysis should treat men and women in the same way (Acker, 1973; Stanworth, 1984); that a woman's work makes a difference to the situation of the family (Britten and Heath, 1983, 1984, Crompton and Jones, 1984); and that the conventional view gives a misleading impression of the occupational structure itself (Crompton and Jones, 1984; Hindess, 1982).

There are several issues at stake in these disputes, only some of which need be dealt with here. Consider first the assumption that the class structure is a structure of families rather than individuals. What is at issue here is a particular notion of class as a socially significant collectivity. In *The Upper Classes*, Scott insists that classes each consist of 'a nexus of interconnected families' (1982, p. 4). 'A particular agent's class situation depends not simply upon his or her "own" life chances, but also on the class situation of the family of origin and on the life chances which the agent's current family is able to pass on to the next generation' (p. 4). Or again, in her discussion of the persistence of the working class family, Humphries (1977) suggests that family loyalties play an important part in generating feelings of solidarity and are a means of transmitting radical sentiments from one generation to the next. In these examples, the family is the means whereby class culture and ideology and the advantages of superior class position may be passed on from one generation to another. Ties of marriage and descent give classes a solidity, in terms of shared attitudes and beliefs and ties of sentiment, that would be lacking if they were considered simply as collections of isolated individuals. I suggested in chapter 3 that one of Goldthorpe's principal concerns with the study of social mobility was its implications for political action through the strengthening or weakening of such collectivities.

If classes are to be considered as collectivities persisting over generations and sharing a common culture, then it makes sense to regard families, rather than individuals, as the basic units. The image here is that of a traditional working class community,

united by the occupational experiences of the men, intergenerational family ties and a common 'class' culture – with the coal-
mining village as perhaps the archetypal case. Of course,
communities of this kind have occupied an important place in the
histories of modern industrial societies. Nevertheless such an
image is only of limited value for the purposes of social analysis. In
particular, it runs together several possible bases of collective
action. It is far from clear why patterns of family ties and shared
culture should be expected to correlate with the occupational
experiences of men. Only when they do correlate can we expect to
find collectivities corresponding to that image of working class
communities.

In other cases we should look for other kinds of collectivity: non-
class communities of various kinds on the one hand, and work-
based collectivities, on the other. Workplace and union
organizations and professional and occupational associations can
provide effective bases of collective action without necessarily
depending on the intergenerational ties and shared culture of the
archetypal working class community. If we are interested in these
kinds of collectivity then, of course, it is individuals, rather than
families, that make up their memberships. An important part of
the dispute over whether classes are made up of families or of
individuals turns on different images of the bases of collective
action. Perhaps, as Garnsey (1978) suggests, we should define class
differently for different purposes of enquiry.

Now consider the second assumption of the conventional view.
If the class structure is a structure of conjugal families why should
we suppose that the class position of a family (and thus of all its
members) is 'determined by the position of that family member
who has, in some sense, the highest level of labour-market
participation' (Goldthorpe, 1984c, p. 497) – in general by the
position of the (male) head of the household? This amounts to
treating the occupational structure (conceived in terms of the
occupations of men) as the key to the class structure (conceived as
a structure of families). One problem here is that the occupational
structure is not in fact a structure of male occupations. In all

industrial societies women make up a significant proportion of the wage-labour force and a large proportion of adult women are now in paid employment. To concentrate on the occupations of men is to disregard several major occupational categories. It is also to ignore those occupational demarcations in which hierarchical relations of authority are mapped on to gender differences in offices, hospitals and other work situations, and where the holders of certain positions (generally men) are routinely serviced by others (almost always women). In their study of clerical work Crompton and Jones note the further point that 'gender itself contributes to the social definition of skill – a minority of jobs are defined as being on the lowest clerical grade, not because of the technical content of the work itself, but rather because the job itself is usually carried out by a woman' (1984, p. 4).

In chapter 4 we noted how Lockwood had modified the weberian tradition of class analysis to include the experience of work as an important dimension of the life chances of individuals. To continue to define class in terms of the occupations of men is then to ignore an important dimension of the work experience of a high proportion of employed women and of many men. In general, the effect of treating the class structure as a structure of families, and then ignoring the work experience of women, is to bring together two conceptions of the social division of labour. On the one hand, there is the division of labour in the economy at large, which, although women do appear in it, is conceived as essentially sexless (i.e. male). On the other hand, there is a division of labour between the roles appropriate to men and women, not only in the family but also in society at large. In this case, the primary social status of the woman is given by her role in the family, while that of the man, and therefore of *his* family, is given by his position in the other division of labour.

Now, an important part of Goldthorpe's defence of the conventional view is that it does accurately reflect the disadvantaged and subordinate position of women in the modern world. Delphy makes the same point in her critique of the treatment of women in stratification studies. The disadvantaged and generally subordinate position of women can hardly be denied, but why should the derivative character of women's class positions follow from it? We have seen that Goldthorpe's position here depends on a limited image of class as a collectivity, and that from a different perspective it may make more sense to regard individuals, rather than families, as the units of class analysis.

But, even if we view the class structure as a structure of families, why should a family's class position be identified with that of the (generally male) head of the household? Several authors have suggested that women's work can make a difference to family behaviour. Crompton and Jones note that 'the employment of women must mean that the "class fates" of many families will be considerably affected by whether the wife is working or not' (1984, p. 130). Receipt of two incomes can have a considerable effect on the pattern of consumption and leisure activities of a family. In the case of some middle class families it can make the difference between payment of school fees and dependence on the state system for a child's education. Similarly, Britten and Heath (1983, 1984) suggest that women's work has implications for voting and other behaviour of family members that cannot be accounted for simply by reference to the husbands' class positions. The 1983 Election Study (Curtice, Heath and Jowell, 1985) also suggests that the occupational position of wives can have significant consequences for the voting behaviour of the members of conjugal families (but see Rose and McAllister, 1986, chapter 3 for a counter-argument).

Perhaps, then, we should follow Britten and Heath and take account of the occupational positions of all members of the family in deciding its class position. Goldthorpe will have none of that: of course, women's work may make a difference but it does not follow that we must therefore abandon the conventional view. Class analysis, in his view, is concerned with the formation of relatively stable collectivities. But if the economic locations of both men and women were taken into account in determining the class positions of families, then we would be left with collectivities of a most insubstantial kind. It would mean that when the implications of the expansion of married women's employment are properly taken into account, the class stratification of contemporary society proves to have a far more fluid form than studies based on the conventional view of the linkage between family and class structure were able to show: the result of women ceasing to be 'peripheral to the class system' has been a remarkable process of class decomposition. (1983, p. 485)

Once again, the image of the class collectivity unified by occupational experiences (of men), intergenerational ties and a shared culture plays a crucial part in Goldthorpe's analysis. A major objective of his defence of the conventional view is to preserve a relatively simple conception of the class structure as a structure of families. If the occupations of both men and women were to be taken into account, then, he maintains, analysis of the class structure would be considerably complicated by the inclusion of relatively impermanent collectivities.

This line of defence fits badly with the professed political motivation of Goldthorpe's mobility study. There he argues that men's experiences of mobility are important because of their consequences for political action through the strengthening or weakening of the shared attitudes, beliefs and ties of sentiment that constitute classes as social realities. Does the generally subordinate position of women mean that their occupational experiences, or lack of them, have no bearing on that political concern? The feminist critique accused much of sociology of being blind to the experiences of women; Goldthorpe's defence of the conventional view seems an excellent case in point. He recognizes the disadvantaged and generally subordinate position of women, and uses that as an excuse for ignoring the political consequences of their occupational experiences.

To conclude, Goldthorpe's defence of the conventional view turns on an image of class as a collectivity united both by the similar occupational experiences of men and by the ties of marriage, descent and a shared culture. There are well known cases of communities in which these elements have gone together to a large extent, but there is no reason to expect them to do so in general. Workplace organizations, trade unions and professional associations have all provided bases of collective action that do not depend on their insertion into 'classes' of the kind that Goldthorpe has in mind. In these cases it is the positions of women and men as individuals that is of primary importance, rather than their positions as members of families. Again, if we are concerned with the positions of families, as units of consumption or the transmission of advantages, there are good reasons for taking the situations of both husbands and wives into account.

These points suggest that class analyses based on the structure of male occupations are, at best, of limited value, and that different conceptions of class may be appropriate for different purposes of enquiry. But there is a further important point to notice here. This book is concerned with those forms of class analysis that insist on the fundamental importance of classes and the relations between them for the understanding of capitalist societies. If classes really are collective actors then we can hardly identify them differently for different purposes of enquiry, as a nexus of interconnected families for some purposes and as collections of individuals for others. If there are different forms of 'class' collective action that might reasonably be described in class terms – depending variously on intergenerational ties and shared culture, workplace organizations, trade unions and professional associations on the one side, and employers' associations, state agencies and the like on the other – can we treat them all as instances of the one underlying class struggle? What is at stake here is the question of reductionism, to which we turn in the next chapter.

6

The Problem of Reductionism

In a letter to Bloch, Engels comments on a recurrent misunderstanding of his and Marx's work:

> According to the materialist conception of history, the *ultimately* determining element in history is the production and reproduction of real life. . . . if somebody twists this into saying that the economic element is the *only* determining one, he transforms that proposition into a meaningless, abstract, senseless phrase. The economic situation is the basis, but the various elements of the superstructure . . . also exercise their influence upon the course of the historical struggles and in many cases preponderate in determining their *form*.
>
> Marx and I are ourselves partly to blame for the fact that the younger people sometimes lay more stress on the economic side than is due to it. We had to emphasise the main principle *vis-à-vis* our adversaries who denied it, and we had not always the time, the place or the opportunity to give their due to the other elements involved in the interaction. (September 21–2, 1890, Marx and Engels, n.d.)

In this letter Engels appears to maintain both that the economic is 'the ultimately determining element in history' and that other, non-economic elements must be given their due. Throughout its history, marxism has been preoccupied with the problem of reconciling these two positions. The problem has generally been regarded as a problem of reductionism. Marxism has been accused by its theoretical opponents of presenting a one-sided, economic interpretation of history. Within marxism the failure to give other elements their due has been denounced as 'economism', that is, as an economic reductionism. Marxists have always insisted that economism is something to be avoided. The great marxist political leaders have always insisted that political struggles are not directly and immediately reducible to classes and their interests. For example, in 'The discussion of self-determination summed up', Lenin attacks as ultra-left the economistic reduction of politics to a simple conflict of classes: 'So one army lines up in one place and says "We are for socialism", and another, somewhere else, and says "We are for capitalism" and that will be a social revolution. . . . whoever expects a "pure" social revolution will *never* live to see it' (1964, pp. 355–6). But Lenin also insisted that political and ideological struggles should be conceptualized in class terms. The base and superstructures model of Marx's Preface to *A Contribution to the Critique of Political Economy* seems to propose a clear reductionist programme, at least on first reading. But, as we saw in chapter 2, there are important respects in which it remains remarkably obscure. Much of post-war marxist theory, at least in the more advanced societies of the capitalist West, has been devoted to developing non-reductionist interpretations of that model.

Economic reductionism is not the only reductionism to be found in the social sciences. A very different kind of reductionism is suggested by the methodological protocols outlined in the early pages of Weber's *Economy and Society*. Weber proposes the reduction of the social realm to the will and consciousness of human individuals. Social relations are intersubjective relations between individuals and social life is the product of their teleological action. Social collectivities, for example, 'must be treated as solely the resultants and modes of organization of the particular acts of individual persons, since these alone can be treated as agents in a course of subjectively understandable action' (Weber, 1968, p. 13). This methodological individualism continues to enjoy a curious respectability in the social sciences, whilst other kinds of reductionism are treated as something to be avoided. Thus, when non-marxist social scientists describe marxism as reductionist they offer not a neutral description but a condemnation. The same applies when marxists describe their marxist opponents as economistic, that is, as practising an economic reductionism. Class or economic reductionism is not only something that social scientists practice, it is also a bad thing.

However, before we go along with the widespread assumption that marxism faces a problem of reductionism a word of warning is in order concerning the notion of reductionism itself. There has been considerable dispute about reductionism in the history and philosophy of the sciences (see James, 1984 for a recent survey). For our purposes the most important point to emerge is that the concept of reduction involved remains somewhat obscure, even in the case of the natural sciences. In social theory, reductionism appears more often as a gesture, to be applauded or condemned as the case may be, than as a serious programme of work. Reductionism in principle is asserted at points in Weber's methodological writings, but it is not seriously followed through in his substantive investigations. As for marxism, there appears to be a reductionist project stated in Marx's 1859 Preface and elsewhere. But for all the various formulations of the idea that the economy does play the ultimately determining role, but only in the last instance, the precise mechanisms of the supposed relationship between economic base and political superstructure are nowhere clearly specified.

This fundamental lack of clarity allows marxists to condemn the economism of others and to maintain, with Engels, that of course other elements must be given their due. Reductionism appears as a problem for marxism because of the inconsistency between a gesture towards a reductionist programme on the one hand and an insistence on the irreducibility of certain crucial phenomena on the other – between the assertion of the ultimately determining role of the economy and the need 'to give their due to the other elements involved' (cf. Johnston, 1986). It has been a recurrent problem because marxism has insisted on maintaining two incompatible accounts of the connections between economic relations and other elements of social life. We consider some of the consequences of that insistence shortly. But it is important to notice that the inconsistencies that give rise to problems of class reductionism are not peculiar to marxism. They are endemic to the project of class analysis itself.

Non-marxist class analysis

While the charge of economic reductionism is often levelled against Marx and marxism, it is almost impossible to level against Weber himself. Weber does propose a reductionist project in his methodological individualism, but, whatever its other problems, that project has no necessary implications for the relationships between the economy and other areas of social life. Weber insists on the importance of a multiplicity of factors in historical explanation, and even where he stresses the role of some particular factor (such as religion) he presents that as a corrective to the one-sided emphasis of marxism. However, the same cannot always be said of 'weberian' class analysis. Before proceeding to the consideration of marxist class analysis it is worth noting that the problematic relationship between class analysis and politics may also be found in the most significant non-marxist alternatives.

In chapter 3 I suggested that a crucial issue for the attempts to develop a non-marxist alternative to marxist class analysis was the existence or otherwise of classes as social realities. The point is to understand the ways in which classes emerge, or fail to emerge, as social realities, to identify the forms of social differentiation that may provide a basis of class formation, and the ties of solidarity and cultural homogeneity that transform such potential classes into 'social realities'. In order to see how such a project can involve problematic relationships between classes and other elements of social life, consider again the works of Giddens, Parkin and Goldthorpe, discussed in chapter 3.

To begin with Giddens, we have seen that he describes a class society as 'one in which class relationships are pre-eminent in the social structure as a whole' (1973, p. 132). In his view the capitalist societies of the modern West are certainly class societies in that sense. In these societies, 'the class system continues to constitute the fundamental axis of the social structure' (p. 294). Class analysis is, therefore, the key to the understanding of politics and culture, and to the identification of the forces engaged in promoting or resisting social change.

Class societies differ considerably amongst themselves. In particular, they differ in 'the specific modes in which class analysis is relevant to the explication of other aspects of the social structure' according to

> (1) The nature and types of class structuration. (2) The nature and types of class consciousness (or class awareness) which correspond to the forms of structuration. (3) The forms assumed by overt class conflict – how far, for example, this is 'institutionalised' as collective bargaining in industry, or as routinised competition between organized class parties in politics. (4) The typical character of class exploitation. (p. 134)

Elsewhere Giddens tells us that 'specifically political influences must be allocated a primary role in interpreting the formation and development of class structures' (p. 21). On the one hand then, class relationships are 'pre-eminent in the social structure as a whole', and on the other, they vary according to social and political factors that cannot be explained in terms of class relationships themselves. Class is 'pre-eminent' yet politics plays 'a primary role'. The details of Giddens's analysis differ from that of Engels, but he clearly follows Engels's lead in trying to have his cake and eat it.

Parkin offers a rather different style of non-marxist class analysis, stressing the role of strategies of social closure rather than social mobility in determining class boundaries. Classes are defined as groupings that may emerge around structural inequalities in society, each type of inequality providing scope for exclusionary or usurpatory forms of collective action. The dominant class is then defined as consisting of those groups whose positions depend primarily on exclusion, while the subordinate class consists of the rest. Parkin's approach certainly avoids the economic reductionism of which marxism is so often accused, since his classes are not defined primarily in terms of economic location, but rather in terms of their modes of collective action. Nevertheless, as we have seen, classes are clearly presented as being the major collective actors in a society, so that the major agencies of organized conflict and of administration are effectively treated as representing classes and their interests.

In effect, we are presented with a model of society in which privileged groups engage in collective action to defend their privileges, while those at the bottom of the social heap try to grab what they can from those above them. Now, there certainly are cases in which privileged groups act collectively to look after their interests, and others in which the less privileged organize against them. But to treat such groups, or classes, as if they were the main political actors is to deny the significance of parties, trade unions, state agencies and all the other movements and organizations that constitute the fields of political struggle in modern societies – except perhaps as 'representing' the classes that underly them. We have seen, for example, how Parkin can reduce the analysis of the state to the identification of the group it represents.

Finally consider Goldthorpe's *Social Mobility and Class Structure in Modern Britain*, already discussed at several points in this book. Goldthorpe's concerns are overtly political. The study of mobility is important because it provides a measure of the degree of 'openness' of a society and especially because the pattern of mobility affects the prospects for radical political action to bring about a more open society. Social mobility is important, then, because of its consequences for the social conditions that foster or inhibit the development of 'the shared beliefs, attitudes and sentiments that are required for concerted class action' (1980, p. 265).

What is so striking about this study is that Goldthorpe draws his conclusions with barely a reference to the organization of British politics and its practices. In spite of his overt concern for the prospects of egalitarian social change in Britain he pays little attention to the political parties, unions and employers' associations, state agencies and other bodies that provide the principal agencies of political struggle in British society, or to the ideologies and forms of political calculation in terms of which these struggles are conducted and political support is mobilized. Instead, like marxism, he proceeds as if 'classes' were really the main political actors in a society, with the result that the primary focus of political analysis concerns the conditions of class formation and action. The specific conditions of organization of parties, trade unions and so on, the ideologies, forms of organization and political calculation available to them are all effectively discounted as being of secondary importance. From this standpoint it makes sense to investigate the concomitants of mobility as if they occurred independently of the activities of political parties, unions, state agencies, the media and so on. Patterns of 'shared beliefs, attitudes and sentiments' can then be treated as if the political work of parties and other agencies, and the struggles within and between them, were of no real importance in the formation of people's concerns and objectives.

There is a clear reductionist premise in this attempt to draw political conclusions from an investigation of the effects of mobility on the conditions of class formation. It requires that things that are not classes, such as state agencies, trade unions and political parties, be treated as if they were classes – or at least as if they represented them. What is at stake here is the refusal to take seriously the consequences of movements and organizations and their actions, both for the construction of political forces and the conditions in which they struggle, and for the formation of the political interests and concerns around which the struggles are conducted. In consequence, political attitudes, beliefs and practices may be regarded as reflecting other social conditions, the implication being that these other conditions are in some sense more real than the political phenomena that reflect them. Like the marxism he rejects, Goldthorpe effectively reduces crucial elements of political life to products of an underlying social reality. In other contexts, of course, Goldthorpe adopts a strenuously anti-reductionist position. We have seen that marxism does the same.

Marxist class analysis

To say that an approach is reductionist and illegitimate is to say that its explanations are incomplete in some important respect. We have just seen that the charge may be levelled against some kinds of weberian class analysis, though not against Weber's own discussion of class. But it has most frequently been made against marxism in general, and by some marxists against others. I have introduced the topic through a discussion of non-marxist class analysis to reinforce the point that the problem is not peculiar to marxism. There are, however, two respects in which marxism is quite distinctive. First, it is openly committed to reductionist principles of explanation (the primacy of class struggle and determination by the economy in the last instance) – and it insists that other elements must be given their due. Secondly, the issue of economism, or economic reductionism, has been a matter of intense and often bitter debate within marxism since its inception. It has been regarded as a matter of vital importance because of the way marxism views the links between theory and politics and it is impossible to discuss marxism without raising the issue of reductionism.

Reductionism has always been recognized as a danger within marxism, and marxists have made numerous more or less sophisticated attempts to show that it can be avoided. One example, noted in chapter 2, is Poulantzas's use of the idea of 'determination in the last instance' by the economy to suggest a certain autonomy of other levels. Others have used the notions of 'relative autonomy' (of the superstructures), 'dialectics', or the difference between 'objective' determinants of class interests and 'subjective' conditions of class consciousness, to similar effect. The point of these and related notions is to indicate that significant elements of politics and culture cannot be understood as directly reflecting divisions at the level of the economy. The claim is that there are indeed connections between the economy and other levels of social organization, but that these connections are often complex and indirect. 'Economism' then is in the failure to acknowledge the complexity of those connections.

In fact the problem for marxism arises not so much from reductionism as from the attempt to combine aparently opposed positions: the economy is the ultimately determining element, but other elements must also be given their due; politics and the state are autonomous, but only relatively so; and so on. Is it possible to develop these gestural accounts of the connections between politics, law and culture on the one hand and the economy and class relations on the other in a way that avoids inconsistency? I return to that question below. For the moment notice that marxist political analysis characteristically operates in two distinct registers, often with little connection between them: there is analysis in terms of the ultimate determinants, and there is analysis that gives other elements their due. Consider some recent examples: first, a commentary on the problems leading to Labour's electoral defeats in 1979 and 1983; secondly, a comparative analysis of post-war social policy in the advanced capitalist societies; and finally, a theoretically sophisticated analysis of the development of socialist and labour movements in the West.

Labour's electoral defeats

Shortly after the 1983 Election the October edition of *Marxism Today* published 'Labour's Lost Millions' by Eric Hobsbawm. Here and in two further pieces (March 1984 and April 1985) Hobsbawm argued that the left in Britain must face up to some unpalatable facts. There had been some significant changes in the British working class since the 1950s and there was now a substantial gap between what Labour, and the left within or close to it, had to offer and the aspirations and concerns of ordinary voters. Some of Hobsbawm's comments generated considerable dispute in the pages of *Marxism Today* and elsewhere, especially his suggestions concerning an anti-Thatcher alliance. However, what concerns us here is not so much the merits or demerits of Hobsbawm's specific proposals, but rather the character of the political analysis from which they are derived.

The first point to notice is that Hobsbawm adopts the characteristic stance of the Communist Party of Great Britain in presuming to tell the Labour Party what it should do. Successive editions of *The British Road to Socialism* (the programme of the CPGB) have justified that stance by means of the claim to a theoretically superior political analysis based on marxism. Hobsbawm does not make that claim explicitly, but his second and third pieces refer to Lenin for support and to Dimitrov's writings of the Popular Front period in the 1930s. His argument makes use of the same theoretical categories as recent editions of *The British Road to Socialism*, and it suffers many of the same weaknesses.

At one level there is a more or less realistic assessment of political conditions − for example, Hobsbawm's comments on voting patterns and on the gap between what Labour appears to offer and the aspirations and concerns of ordinary people. Much of what Hobsbawm has to say at this level is sensible, if rather limited. At a second level is the discussion of social forces, notably, 'the working class as a whole' and the various social categories that are supposed to be its potential allies: 'the women', 'the minority nations and ethnic minorities', 'the intellectuals'. What is striking in Hobsbawm's argument, as in *The British Road to Socialism*, is that there is very little connection between these two levels of analysis. Reference to 'the working class' as a social force and to the other categories that are to be allied with it is mostly empty sloganizing. To be told that 'Labour must recover the support of the working class as a whole' adds nothing at all to what is sensible and realistic in Hobsbawm's discussion of the gap between the Labour Party and millions of voters.

The details of Hobsbawm's analysis have been disputed by other marxists. But his essays do exhibit a combination of more or less realistic assessment of political conditions with 'analysis' of the class and other forces that are supposed to underly them. This combination is all too characteristic of political thinking on the left. Class analysis on the British left, far from illuminating the problems that socialists have to confront, is an obstacle to the serious analysis of political conditions that is so badly needed. The refusal to face up to unpleasant facts is indeed a problem on the left – as it is elsewhere in British politics – and Hobsbawm is right to challenge it. Unfortunately in retaining the categories of a simplistic marxism he avoids the more serious task of challenging the left to face up to fundamental flaws in the way it conducts its political analysis.

What is at stake in this treatment of 'the working class as a whole' and other categories as unities for the purposes of political analysis is the idea that membership of a class or category (Hobsbawm refers to 'all women' and 'all young people') defines an interest, irrespective of whether the individuals concerned recognize that interest as their own. This idea is the foundation of all that is most fantastic in the British left's assessment of its potential support. In particular, it allows many on the left both to admit that their policies have little popular support and to insist that they should not be changed – precisely because they do correspond to the real interests of the working class and the mass of the British people. Hobsbawm castigates the patronizing attitude of much of the left towards the aspirations and concerns of the British people, but then comes dangerously close to such an attitude himself whenever he derives an interest from membership of a social category. At one point, for example, he identifies 'all who want democracy, a better and fairer society' with 'all workers by hand and brain'. Perhaps all workers *should* be committed to democracy and fairness, but there is precious little evidence that they are. Support for the principles of democracy and fairness has to be won and sustained against powerful anti-egalitarian sentiments and institutional arrangements in British society. It cannot be assumed to follow simply from membership of the working class or of one of the other categories that are supposed to be its allies.

Social policy in the advanced capitalist societies

An early comparative study by Wilensky (1975) had suggested that the primary determinants of welfare expenditure were the level of economic development and the demographic structure of the population. On that account, differing political ideologies had relatively little impact. This conclusion has been disputed in recent years by several authors who argue that the development of social policy should be seen as the product of conflicting class forces (Clegg et al., 1986; Esping-Anderson, 1985; Korpi, 1983; Stephens, 1979). In effect, two theses are involved in this argument. One is that the level of welfare expenditure is an unsatisfactory index of the character of social policy, since welfare states differ in the institutional structure of welfare provision and also, for example, in the extent to which it is universalistic and redistributive. The second is that classes have differing interests in the institutional character of social policy and they therefore pursue rather different policy objectives. The institutional character of social policy can then be seen, in part, as the outcome of struggles between contending classes.

The argument has been advanced in a number of rather different forms and it raises important issues, some of which are discussed in the final chapter. For the moment, consider the version advanced by Esping-Anderson and Korpi. Social policy is to be seen as an outcome of conflict and bargaining between classes. It therefore depends on the strategies or tactics employed by the contending collectivities and on the power resources available to them. Esping-Anderson and Korpi maintain that the two principal types of power resources in capitalist societies are the 'ownership of capital' and 'the labour-power and numbers of wage-earners'. These resources may be used more or less effectively, and there are costs associated with their use.

> The effectiveness of these power resources can be increased through organizations for collective action, such as juristic persons, business organizations, political parties, and labour

unions. To decrease the costs associated with the use of power resources, it is advantageous to invest resources in attempts to shape institutions for decision-making and for the regulation of the behaviour of citizens. (Esping-Anderson and Korpi, 1984, p. 182)

In effect, organizations for collective action are instruments of class action. At one level of analysis there are the various contending classes, and at another level there are organizations for collective action and the institutional structures they have shaped. Detailed discussion of policy development operates at the second level, since it is parties, unions and the like that actually bargain and pursue strategies. But these are always referred back to the primary level, to the classes that are supposed to underly them. What this adds to the analysis in terms of organizations and movements is the principle of their explanation. Political strategies for the development of social policy are seen, in other words, as reflecting the interests of classes or as compromises resulting from class-alliances. Here too class interests are seen as objectively given in the structure of capitalist relations and as having real political effects. I argue in the following chapter that such uses of 'interests' obscure far more than they explain. This brings us to my final example.

The development of socialist and labour movements in the West

If the limitations of the arguments of Hobsbawm and of Esping-Anderson and Korpi stem from their rather different treatments of interests as objectively given, perhaps they could be avoided by a more sophisticated marxism. Przeworski's analysis of the development of socialist and labour movements in the advanced capitalist societies explicitly rejects the idea that class interests are an objective and unproblematic basis for collective action. Instead classes are themselves treated as outcomes of struggles which have the organization, reorganization and disorganization of classes as effects. Position in the relations of production, then, cannot suffice to define a class interest. Rather, interests are seen as constituted by specific 'strategies of class formation' (Przeworski, 1977, p. 401) as these are implemented more or less successfully in the course of struggle.

Once again, we are concerned with the character of the theoretical tools that Przeworski employs rather than with the details of his analysis. There is an obvious question regarding his concept of class. We can agree that the formation of collectivities and agencies of struggle should be analysed as a consequence of specific social conditions and struggles, but why should we also assume that the most important agencies of struggle will turn out to be *classes*? Why, in other words, should unities conceived as in some way related to the organization of production be considered the most significant collective actors and agencies of struggle? By way of answer, Przeworski simply refers us to his commitment to a notion of history as ultimately directed by the development of productive forces and capital accumulation. The primacy of class over other struggles is therefore given by the character of society as ultimately governed by the productive forces. In effect, Przeworski's answer returns us to the model sketched in Marx's 1859 Preface. The character of the economy determines the main lines of political struggle. In the case of capitalist societies this means that political struggle is ultimately between capitalism and socialism, between bourgeoisie and proletariat. Political and ideological conditions may play a part in the formation of specific collectivities and agencies of struggle, but they do not affect what the struggle is ultimately about.

Przeworski's political analysis, then, also operates on two levels. It gives other elements their due while ensuring that they are somehow constrained to operate within the main lines of struggle laid down by the economy. At one level is the analysis of socialist and labour movements in terms of their formation under specific economic, political and ideological conditions. There is no question here of any simplistic derivation of interests from class position of the kind that mars Hobsbawm's 'Labour's Lost Millions' and much of the subsequent debate. At the other level is yet another version of the ultimately determining role of the economy. Since the struggle is about the maintenance or over-throw of capitalism then, as Johnston points out (1986, p. 107), class formation is a problem only for the forces of change, that is, only for the proletariat. On the one side, (the proletariat) class formation depends on specific social conditions and strategies of class formation. On the other, the bourgeoisie derives its capacities not from specific social conditions but rather from the overall structure of the capitalist totality.

Conclusion

To conclude this chapter, consider what it is that class analysis pretends to tell us about politics. Neither marxism nor the non-marxist advocates of class analysis considered above seriously maintain that class analysis tells us all we need to know about the political forces at work in a given society and the struggles between them. When we examine the forces engaged in particular struggles, we do not find *classes* in the literal sense, lined up against each other. Instead we find political parties and factions within them, trade unions, employers and employers organizations, newspapers and television companies (and factions within them), state agencies, and a variety of other organizations and individ-uals. If class relationships are indeed 'pre-eminent in the social structure as a whole', as Giddens suggests (1973, p. 132), then class analysis should allow us to make sense of the multiplicity of agencies and forms of struggle that appear in political life.

In effect, the promise that class analysis offers to our under-standing of politics presupposes the existence of two distinct but related levels of analysis. At the first level are factions, parties, movements and the like and the doctrines and ideologies in terms of which they mobilize support and organize their conduct. Secondly, there is the more fundamental level that provides the key to our understanding of the first. This more fundamental level of analysis may be conceived in various ways, as our examples have shown. But in all cases the class analysis of politics involves the following features. First, there are two assumptions:

1 The two levels of analysis really are distinct. It follows that there must be significant elements of the first level not wholly determined by the second.
2 Analysis at the second, more fundamental level tells us something essential about the first. For example, it identifies interests (Hobsbawm and most forms of marxist political analysis), the main lines of political struggle in capitalist society (Przeworski) or the prospects for egalitarian political change (Goldthorpe).

The third common feature is a merely gestural connection between the two levels of analysis. Class analysis, in other words, promises to combine an insistence on the irreducibility of political life with the promise of reductionism. But how the trick is done remains obscure.

In *Marx's Capital and Capitalism Today* (Cutler et al., 1977, 1978) my co-authors and I argued that marxist attempts to avoid the dangers of reductionism were ultimately unsuccessful. Marxist political analysis supposes a relationship between the economy and politics, between the distribution of the population into classes and political organizations, institutions and ideologies, that combines the ultimately determining role of the one with the irreducibility of the other. There must be effective non-class and non-economic elements of political life whose effects are nevertheless ultimately constrained to conform to the ultimately determining role of the economy: they must be autonomous, but only relatively so. The problem is that the precise mechanisms of the relationship that is supposed to hold between the economic base and political superstructure are nowhere clearly specified.

Marx's Capital and Capitalism Today argued that there was no coherent way in which politics could be conceived as strictly irreducible to the economy, while at the same time the economy was conceived as playing the ultimately determining role. 'Determination in the last instance', 'relative autonomy' and related notions are merely gestures towards the solution of a problem that cannot be resolved. Indeed, their effectiveness as solutions requires that they remain no more than gestures – suggesting that inconsistency can be avoided without in fact showing that it can be done. Otherwise, they revert to a direct reductionism of precisely the kind they are intending to avoid, or else they effectively deny the primacy of class struggle and the economy.

In fact, these problems are in no way peculiar to marxism. They are generated by the promise that class analysis, marxist or otherwise, pretends to offer for our understanding of political life. We have seen that non-marxist class analysis slides somewhat uneasily between two levels of political analysis. Like the marxism it is so careful to reject, it offers a reductionism on the one hand and an insistence on the irreducible significance of politics on the other. Nevertheless, marxism has consistently shown a greater awareness of the issues than have the alternative forms of class analysis. How has marxism responded to the charge that the assertion of the ultimately determining role of the economy cannot be coherently combined with an affirmation of the real autonomy of politics? Stuart Hall's response to an earlier version of the argument will suffice – but see also the review by Harris (1978) and our reply (Cutler et al., 1979). Hall admits that there are indeed dangers of reductionism and argues that they can be avoided. To the argument that there is no correspondence between politics and the economy of the kind required by the ultimately determining role of the latter he replies: 'To suggest that they are not articulated, that there is no "correspondence" of any kind, is to forfeit the first principle of historical materialism: the principle of the social formation as a "complex unity" . . . But that articulation is accomplished only through a series of displacements and disarticulations' (1978, p. 47). A few pages later he suggests that the notion of society as a complex unity is essential to marxism, but that it is 'a unity which is not a simple or reductionist one' (p. 58). In reply to the argument that 'determination in the last instance' and all the other slogans are nothing more than gestures, we are offered yet another gesture. After more than 100 years of marxist theory the time has surely come to establish the mechanisms of the supposed ultimately determining role of the economy, which manage nevertheless to respect the autonomy of politics, rather than merely to assert that they exist.

Politics and Class Analysis

What then remains of the class analysis of politics? After considering several areas of difficulty for the most influential forms of class analysis, I argued in chapter 6 that the appeal of class analysis rests on a promise that is little more than a gesture, and further, that it cannot in fact be fulfilled. Nevertheless there are groups in all societies in the modern world who do analyse politics and act at least in part on those terms. The significance of these groups varies of course from one society to another and over time. But forms of politics involving class analysis have some support in most societies and in some cases they have been extremely influential. There are numerous social movements and political struggles that appear to indicate the pertinence of classes and the idea of class struggle in modern history – for example, the role of socialist and class-based movements throughout Western Europe in the nineteenth and early twentieth centuries and, in some cases, to an extent that remains significant today. Surely, it might be argued, the persistence of movements organized at least in part around ideas of class struggle and the strength of some of them suggest that class analysis cannot be dismissed quite so easily?

Perhaps, but we should be careful not to confuse questions of the political significance of class analysis with questions of its validity. (Few in the West would claim that the political significance of Shiite Islam demonstrates its validity as a mode of political analysis.) In a famous passage near the beginning of *The Communist Manifesto*, Marx and Engels insist that history 'is the history of class struggles' (1968 p. 35) and the imagery of class struggle is a ubiquitous feature of class analysis, marxist and non-marxist. It suggests that classes are things that engage in struggle with each other, and perhaps with other things as well. How is that suggestion to be understood? Are classes themselves collective actors or should we understand the notion of class struggle as a shorthand reference to something altogether more complex?

To bring that question into sharper focus, consider some more recent cases of class analysis. In chapter 6 I referred to a comparative argument relating the development of social policy in the advanced capitalist societies to the balance of class forces. Briefly, the argument is that while the overall level of welfare expenditure may, as Wilensky (1975) argued, reflect a society's demographic profile and its level of economic development, classes have differing interests in the institutional character of social policy and can be expected to pursue different policy objectives. The development of social and economic policy will therefore depend on the organizational and other resources at the disposal of the contending classes, and on the success of the tactics they employ. Where there is a high degree of unionization and the labour movement is unified, then it may be able to bargain with government as well as with employers – for example, by offering reduced industrial militancy in return for an improved social wage and the preservation of high levels of employment.

The prospects for such a strategy depend on the ability of the working class to pursue it in a unified fashion and, of course, on the opposing forces. If the latter are strong and well organized, then the rewards of working class restraint may be rather limited. If the level of unionization is low, or if there are serious sectional divisions, then the labour movement will be in a weaker position *vis-à-vis* government, and less able to pursue a coherent strategy of any kind. The capitalist class on the other hand, has a clear interest in a weak labour movement and in promoting sectional divisions within it. It is not surprising, then, that in Western Europe at the present day, it would be difficult to find instances in which it could be plausibly held that corporatist institutions are being sustained in the interests of capital – for example, by right-wing government and representatives of employers; but easy to find ones in which the latter have openly rejected corporatism, in the sense of concertation, or are seeking in one way or another to undermine it. (Goldthorpe, 1984a, p. 13)

Contrary to a view that is widely held on the English-speaking left (e.g., Panitch, 1986), the argument is that the working class have more to gain from the effects of entering into corporatist arrangements with government and capital than it would lose by having to curb its industrial militancy. The point can be illustrated by reference to employment policy: 'Among the Western nations since 1973, it is only the three with the most powerful labour movement – Sweden, Norway, and Austria – which have utilized macro-economic, wage- or labour-market policies in order to hold unemployment at relatively low levels' (Esping-Anderson and Korpi, 1984, p. 205; cf. Therborn, 1986). Whether the working class can impose such an arrangement and what it stands to gain from it will depend, of course, on the relative strengths of the different classes. But where the working class is successful in this respect, then corporatist arrangements can be expected to lead, as in Sweden, in the direction of further radical shifts in social policy and the development of public controls over investment.

Now, I have considerable sympathy with this argument, although I shall be critical of important elements within it. It raises important theoretical and political issues and it has been developed in a number of different versions (Clegg, Boreham and Dow, 1986; Esping-Anderson, 1985; Goldthorpe (ed.), 1984; Korpi, 1983; Stephens, 1979), some of them far more sophisticated than my brief account might suggest. One respect in which they differ is in the treatment of classes as social forces, and it is this aspect that I concentrate on here. Several authors proceed as if concepts of class interests and classes as social forces were relatively unproblematic. Esping-Anderson and Korpi, for example, write as if classes were themselves collectivities engaged in struggle, who have developed parties, unions and other organizations, and attempted to shape public institutions, in order to further their collective interests. Parties can then be seen as representing classes, class fractions and alliances between them, and their class interests as given in the basic structures of the economy. With regard to social policy, the overriding concerns of the working class parties have been to reduce workers' dependence on market forces by developing a system of basic citizenship rights and maintaining full employment. The aim here is both to protect the material interests of the working class and to develop its forces for further action. 'Social policy institutions that compartmentalized occupational groups, status categories, or classes would easily consolidate traditional lines of cleavage and even create new, separate interests. This, in turn, would induce competition rather than nurture solidarity. A universalistic strategy should help to promote the mobilization of the largest possible number of citizens for collective action' (Esping-Anderson and Korpi, 1984, p. 184). The bourgeois forces, on the other hand, have an interest in limiting the political and economic strength of the working class. This means that they tend to favour decentralized wage-bargaining and forms of social policy that promote sectional divisions – for example, by dividing wage-earners into distinct occupational groups, separating manual workers from other employees and fostering the growth of private pension and insurance schemes.

Here the classes are conceived as having underlying interests given in the structure of capitalist society which they pursue to the best of their abilities according to the forces at their disposal and the forces they have to contend with. Other authors are more circumspect, especially about the conceptualization of class and their interests. For example, Clegg, Boreham and Dow insist that interests cannot be said to exist prior to their articulation in some form: 'Without organization there can be no "class interests". The notion of a class having a collective interest can only ever gain credence inasmuch as organizations are formed whose mandate entails the representation of "class interests"' (1986, pp. 259–60). The implication here is that parties, unions and other organizations cannot be seen as mere instruments in the pursuit of some pre-defined set of interests. In particular, they are not in any straightforward sense the means of action of a class – since the 'interests' they articulate and pursue are not given in advance. Nevertheless, Clegg, Boreham and Dow continue to write of classes as themselves engaged in struggle for 'greater control over the capitalist system as a whole (in the long term, the stakes are somewhat higher of course)' (p. 259).

Or again, Goldthorpe insists that interests should not be regarded as sociological givens: 'the function of representative organizations is not merely to express, but actually to formulate interests, in response to pressure from both their memberships and from their bargaining partners, *and also in the light of their leaders' own conceptions of appropriate strategies*' (1984b, p. 236, emphasis added). Goldthorpe's point about 'leaders own conceptions' means that organizations cannot be seen as the mere instrumentalities of a class. Nevertheless, he insists that the political bargaining of unions in the context of corporatist arrangements is 'far more evidently oriented towards specifically *class* interests than is "free" collective bargaining of a conventional kind (no matter how militant) in which sectional interests are typically involved and often dominant' (1984a, p. 13). These examples may refer to classes and their interests in rather different ways, but they all raise a similar set of questions. What are these 'classes' and 'class interests' and how do they produce their effects? What do they have to offer by way of explanation of the behaviour of parties, unions and other organizations or, for that matter, of human individuals? Perhaps the classes themselves are collective actors, or perhaps the idea of classes as social forces should be understood in a different way – in terms of the class interests they pursue. After discussion of these suggestions, this final chapter argues that classes are not social forces at all. Discussion of politics in terms of class struggle is at best a rather complex allegory and at worst thoroughly misleading.

Classes as collective actors

Consider first the idea that a class is a particular kind of collective actor. To see what is involved here we need to be clear about what is minimally required for something to be called an actor (Hindess, 1986a). An actor is a locus of decision and action, where the action is in some sense a consequence of the actor's decisions. Actors' decisions play a part in the explanation of their actions. Actors may also do things that are not a consequence of decisions, and they require a different form of explanation, but this aspect of the matter need not concern us here. Reference to an actor, then, always presupposes some definite means of reaching and formulating decisions, definite means of acting on them, and some connections between the two. Human individuals are certainly actors in this sense, but they are clearly not the only things that reach decisions and act accordingly. Capitalist enterprises, state agencies, political parties and trade unions are all examples of actors other than human individuals. They all have means of reaching and formulating decisions and of acting on at least some of them. Call these things 'social actors'.

Can classes be regarded as social actors in this sense? An actor is something that formulates decisions and acts on some of them, and I have just given several examples of social actors. Difficulties arise, however, when the concept of actor is extended to collectivities, such as 'classes', 'societies', 'men' (considered as a collectivity subordinating 'women' as another collectivity), that have no identifiable means of formulating decisions, let alone of acting on them. Unlike capitalist enterprises or political parties, which have definite means of reaching and formulating decisions, classes and societies all too clearly do not. Of course, there will always be those who claim to make decisions and to act on behalf of classes and other collectivites. However, the very diversity of such claims is reason to be sceptical about identifying any one of them with the decisions of the collectivity in question.

Now the reason for restricting the concept of actor to a thing that formulates decisions and acts on them is that actors' decisions play an important part in the explanation of their actions. To extend the concept of actor to collectivities that have no means of formulating decisions and then to treat what happens as resulting from their decisions, is to provide a spurious explanation. To treat the development of social policy as resulting from the strategies of classes and the struggles between them, as in the arguments outlined above, would be to bring together a variety of agencies, struggles and social conditions into a series of imaginary unities, namely the contending classes considered here as actors. That may be a way of suggesting that changes are desirable, but it tells us nothing about how they may be brought about. The invocation of spurious actors in this way may serve a polemical function, but it thoroughly obscures understanding of the social conditions and processes in question and political decisions as to what can or should be done about them.

Reference to classes as actors, then, is not to be taken literally. It is allegorical at best, presenting us with a complex story in the guise of something simpler, and at worst thoroughly misleading. There are indeed social actors, some of which play an important part in the societies of the modern world, but classes are not among them. Class struggle must therefore be understood, if it is to be understood at all, not as a matter of collective *actors* fighting amongst themselves but rather as a shorthand reference to something more complex. It is for this reason that the treatment of classes as social forces normally involves an analysis that operates on two levels, as we saw in chapter 6.

Class interests

Now consider the suggestion that the idea of classes as social forces should be understood in a different way – in terms of a concept of class interests. Marxism provides the best known examples of such a conception of interests, but it can also be found in non-marxist versions of class analysis. In its simplest form the idea is that class interests are given in the structure of social relations (Marx's relations of production, Dahrendorf's authority relations, or whatever) and the parties, unions, factions and other diverse agencies of political life should be seen as their more or less adequate representations. We have seen that there may be more complicated accounts of classes and their interests, but in general the idea of conflicting class interests seems to allow us to bring together a variety of particular struggles into a larger pattern. The underlying distribution of interests then provides the key to understanding the surface phenomena of political life.

Now, the claim that such 'interests' perform an explanatory role returns us to the issue noted above, namely, that of the mechanisms linking those interests to the political behaviour either of human individuals or of parties, unions and other organizations. In the case of human individuals it might seem plausible to suggest that the interests themselves provide an explanatory link between action and social structure: on the one hand they provide us with reasons for action and on the other they are derived from features of social structure. Actors, in this view, have interests by virtue of the conditions in which they find themselves, as members of a class, gender, age group or community. Different features of those conditions may then be seen as giving rise to different, and possibly conflicting, sets of interests. The identification of such cross-pressures has been an important theme in several traditions of political analysis – and it can also be found in Wright's analysis of contradictory class locations (1978).

Unfortunately, such an approach leaves us with no account of the mechanisms whereby parties, unions or state agencies can be said to act in terms of class interests, and it is unsatisfactory even in the case of human individuals. To establish these points it will be necessary to reconsider first the place of interests and related concepts in the explanation of action, and secondly their relation to social structure. I shall argue that in so far as interests have an explanatory role, they are always dependent on definite discursive and other kinds of conditions, and their identification is always open to dispute. Interests are not fixed or given properties of individuals or groups, and they should not be regarded as structurally determined. The claim that class as a social force can be understood in terms of the representation of class interests must therefore collapse.

Interests and reasons for action

The notion of real interests is widely used in political discussion. An influential American textbook goes so far as to assert that 'every explanatory theory of politics includes somewhere in its structure assumptions about persons and their real interests' (Connolly, 1983, p. 73). Interests may be invoked to provide justification for actions said to be performed on behalf of others. For example, children, the elderly and the insane are often regarded as having, at best, a limited capacity to recognize what their interests really are, thereby providing the rationale for the interventions of relatives and 'caring' professionals. Or again, political parties and factions within them may claim to act in the real interests of a class or community. But the most common usage of interests is as an explanation of political behaviour, and it is this usage that concerns us here.

I argue, contrary to Connolly's claim, that the assumption of real interests is an obstacle to the development of adequate explanations. If the concept of interests is to play any part in the analysis of action it can only be because interests are thought to relate to the decisions of particular actors, and therefore to their actions. Actors formulate decisions and act on some of them. The concept of interests refers to some of the reasons that may come in to the process of formulating a decision, to act or to do nothing, to support some policy or party, to oppose it or to abstain, and so on. Actors' decisions may relate to their own interests or to the interests of others, and they may relate to reasons of other kinds, to values, sudden impulses or whatever. What matters here, of course, is not that the word 'interests' should appear in the formulation of reasons for a decision. Interests can also be said to provide reasons for a decision if the reasons that are formulated relate to the benefit or well-being of some actor or actors. The interests of employees in a factory may be said to be involved in a decision to resist its closure, even if the word 'interests' is not used in their deliberations.

Interests are effective in so far as they they provide reasons for actors' decisions. Two aspects of this conception of the connection between interests and action are important here. First, interests are effective, in the sense of having social consequences, only as conceptions: that is, they must be formulated or reflected in reasons that are formulated if they are to be acted upon. If they provide no actor with reasons for action they have no social consequences. This point may seem trivial, but we shall see that it has important consequences for the ways in which interests may be said to have political repercussions.

Secondly, interests not only provide reasons that enter into some process of assessment, but they are also, at least in principle, products of assessment themselves. If they are to provide reasons for action it must be possible to present them as the outcome to some process of assessment ('this strike is in the interests of the miners because . . .'). What is involved here is the construction of an account of the actors' situation and of how they might be affected by particular changes or actions. In many situations a variety of distinct and competing ways of assessing the interests of specific actors or groups of actors will be available. Because they are products of assessments, interests are always potentially open to dispute and the interests of particular actors may be differently identified by the actors concerned and other agencies, or by the same actors at different times. What does this imply for the use of interests in social analysis?

Consider the question of what interests are or may be effective in particular sites of action, social relations or struggles. The first point to notice is that this question has nothing to do with questions of the accuracy or 'validity' of the interests in question. Interests are effective, in the sense of having social consequences, not because they are valid, but rather because of the part they play in the reaching of decisions by some actor or actors. In the 1984–5 miners' strike in Britain, for example, distinct and conflicting conceptions of the interests of the miners were effective. The miners' interests had been at issue in the decisions of miners who supported the strike and in the decisions of miners who opposed it. Which position was correct was itself a matter of dispute, and the conduct of that dispute had consequences in the changing pattern of support for the opposed positions – but it was not the 'validity' or 'objectivity' of one set of interests rather than another that determined what support it had.

The interests that have social consequences are not always those acknowledged by the actors to whom they are attributed, and it is not the validity of the attribution that secures their effectiveness. To say that interests are effective in so far as they provide reasons for action is to say that those reasons are articulated by particular agencies, by individuals or by organizations such as governments, trade unions or political parties. The interests involved in the reasons they articulate may be their own or ones they attribute to others. Trade unions may, for example, calculate their own interests and those of their members, and they may also calculate the interests of various other constituencies, the labour movement, the working class, the unemployed, etc. Other agencies may also claim to identify the interests of those constituencies and to act in pursuit of them. There is no reason to suppose that the interests of the unions or their members as calculated by these various agencies will coincide, still less that they will necessarily correspond to assessments of their interests by union members themselves. Indeed, there have been well known cases where the politics of a union are contrary to those of a majority of their members.

To say that interests depend on forms of assessment is to say also that they are not arbitrary or a matter of entirely free choice. Interests are effective only in so far as they play a part in the formulation of actors' decisions. Actors make decisions and try to act on them, but that does not mean that there are no limits to what they are able to decide, that they can always do what they have decided to do, or that they can decide to do anything. The decisions they formulate and the reasons that enter into those decisions depend on the discursive means available to them, and actors have very little choice over what those means are. Actors may work to change how they think, but they cannot adopt new discursive forms at will. Consider again the example of the 1984–5 miners' strike. The claims of those miners who supported the strike and the claims of those who opposed it involved assessments of miners' interests that were far from arbitrary. Both sets of interests were products of definite modes of assessment of what the miners' interests were, which were themselves well established in mining communities in Britain. Both could provide reasons for decisions within the decisionmaking procedures of the miners' union. Other conceptions of the miners' interests were certainly possible, but to be effective they would have had to provide possible reasons within the current means of reaching decisions and of assessing what their interests were.

Actors are clearly limited in the extent to which they can choose the forms of assessment employed by or available to them. But that is not to say that those forms of assessment are uniquely determined by their social location. In many contexts the forms of assessment available to actors allow the formulation of a variety of distinct and conflicting reasons, objectives and decisions. This possibility provides considerable scope for dispute and also for the persuasion, propaganda and other forms of political work intended to change people's assessments of their interests and how they might be served. What interests or reasons for action are acknowledged in any given case depends not only on the forms of assessment available to the actors, but also on other conditions, including the work of individuals, political parties, unions and other agencies, in support of some assessment of interests and against others.

Finally, I have insisted that questions of what interests are effective should not be confused with questions of their validity, in the sense of corresponding to some objectively determined real interests. But there is a different sense in which it may well be reasonable to question the correctness of the attribution of interests. The point here is that the attribution of interests implies the claim that those whose interests they are said to be will benefit in some way from their successful pursuit. The validity of such claims is of obvious importance to political actors (including many social scientists). They are open to question in at least two respects: there is, first, the question of whether the supposed benefits are really benefits at all, and, secondly, the question of whether they are likely to be realized by pursuit of the interests specified. In some cases there may be clear and unambiguous answers to such questions. There would not be much dispute, for example, about the claim that the interests of the British people are served by the maintenance of elementary public health measures. But in general the attribution of interests is not so clear-cut. Returning to the arguments considered at the beginning of this chapter, the claim that corporatist arrangements are in the interests of the working class could be questioned by asking whether the increased social wage and higher employment were worth the sacrifices that corporatism requires of the working class, and also whether corporatism would actually deliver the goods. An important part of political debate consists of disputes over the attribution of interests and how they might best be pursued. They can have significant effects on the balance of political forces around the issues in dispute – and sometimes more generally when the disputed issues are part of a wider ideological polarization.

Interests and social relations

Perhaps the most common approach to the explanation of interests is to locate them in terms of some concept of social structure. Actors have interests as a consequence of their position as members of a group or class in relation to members of other groups or classes. Most forms of marxism analyse the distribution of interests in terms of a structure of class relations, which in turn is largely a function of definite relations of production. Sociological critics of marxism, such as Dahrendorf and Parkin, see the structure of class relations rather differently, but continue to account for interests in class terms. Others analyse the distribution of interests in terms of group rather than class membership. These positions share a view of interests as reflecting an actor's location within a structure of social relations. The concept of interests then appears to provide an explanatory link between structural location and an actor's behaviour.

There are several reasons why the notion of interests as given by or reflecting social structural location is unsatisfactory. Consider first the notion of real interests – interests that are supposed to have an objective reality but are not necessarily recognized by those whose interests they are thought to be. If they are not recognized then they cannot provide those actors with reasons for action: interests that are real but unrecognized provide reasons for action only in the case of other actors, who may claim to recognize the interests without necessarily sharing them. Real interests in this case are ascribed to those for whom they do not provide reasons for action. Concepts of interests that are real but not recognized by those they are ascribed to may well have social effects – for example, in the actions of political parties and sects, the decisions of parents, teachers or social workers – but they provide no explanatory link between the social location of actors and their actions.

Such cases apart, we are concerned with interests in so far as they relate to the decisions of particular actors, and therefore to their actions. How far can interests that actors recognize as their own be explained as reflecting their social location? I have argued that if interests are to provide reasons for action it must be possible to present them as the outcome of some process of assessment. There are two kinds of problem here for the view of interests as reflecting social location. First, the forms of assessment available to actors are not uniquely determined by their social location. It follows that the interests actors recognize and act upon cannot be uniquely determined by social location either. Secondly, in considering actors' reasons for action we are not generally concerned with the deliberations of perfectly rational actors.

Unlike the idealized puppets of rational choice theory, actors' deliberations are rarely completely programmed by the form of assessment employed in any given case (Hindess, 1984). Their conclusions are reached through complex internal processes, which may vary from one actor to another and within the same actor over time.

If interests are not mere transmissions between social structure and action, there are nevertheless various ways in which actors' social location may relate to the interests, desires or beliefs they are able to formulate. First, individuals may differ with regard to the forms of assessment available to them at any given time. For example, the use of specialized medical and other professional discourses often requires specialist training and the occupation of particular professional positions. More generally, the cultural and educational diversity of most societies ensures that there will be a differential availability of means of assessing their situation. Secondly, if certain actors are unable to locate themselves in relation to the conditions in which they find themselves in terms of a particular discourse, then they are unlikely to employ that discourse to identify their interests. For example, accountants and members of other professional groups may find it difficult to locate themselves in terms of a class-based socialist discourse. Similarly, female part-time workers may have some difficulty locating themselves in relation to trades union discourses conducted in terms of some notion of the 'family wage'. Or again, if interests provide actors with reasons for action, then the interests they formulate will depend on the possibilities for action that they believe to be available to them. All employees in a manufacturing enterprise may be affected by its investment strategy, but they are not equally well placed to act upon it. Finally, actors will be differentially affected by social conditions and changes within them. To continue with my last example, senior managers and wage-labourers in the same company can be expected to formulate rather different interests with regard to investment strategies both because they have very different means of acting on them and because they will be affected differentially.

Class analysis and politics

Where do these arguments leave us? Analyses of politics in terms of the struggle between competing classes usually involve some combination of two elements, both of which I have disputed. One is the notion of classes as actors, and the other the conception of class interests as objectively given in the structure of society. I have argued that there are indeed actors other than human individuals, but that classes are not among them. For that reason alone (there are many others) the analysis of politics in terms of struggle between classes, in the sense of collective actors, must be regarded as highly problematic.

What of the view that classes as social forces should be understood rather as a variety of distinct agencies unified in terms of the class interests they represent? I have argued that interests should not be regarded as given by or reflecting social structural location. Interests have consequences in so far as they provide some actor or actors with reasons for action. The 'objectivity' of those interests, or their lack of it, has no bearing on that issue. Conceptions of interests that are real or objective but not recognized by those they are ascribed to may well have consequences – in the actions of political parties and others who claim to represent those interests – but they provide no explanatory link between the social location of those actors and their actions.

Nevertheless, I have suggested several respects in which actors' situations may be connected with their beliefs and the interests that they recognize and act upon. Two of these seem particularly worth noting here. First, the formulation of interests involves actors in the assessment of the conditions they confront and in locating themselves and others in relation to those conditions and possible changes in them. In this respect much of the conceptual purchase of class analysis is a function of its reference to pervasive features of property and employment relations in the modern world. By the same token, part of the continued weakness of class politics is a function of the difficulty of conceptualizing in class terms the growth since the late nineteenth century of impersonal forms of property and the employment of those who do not fall readily into the categories of capitalist or exploited wage-labourer. We have seen that contemporary class analysis is much concerned with these issues.

Secondly, of course, class analysis is far from being the only mode of political assessment available to actors in the modern world. If we are concerned with the ways in which reference to class struggle and class interests function as components of certain movements and practices – for example, in the mobilization of support and in decisions as to political strategy – we must also consider other modes of political assessment. Those who do conduct their politics in class terms have both to compete and work together with adherents of other versions of class analysis and with agencies who conduct their politics in terms of other modes of assessment – in terms of individualism, nationalism, religious and other sectional divisions, and so on. Support for different ways of conducting and analysing politics is one of the outcomes of competition between them. It is never simply a reflection of social structure. The relative strength or weakness of class-based forms of politics in, say, Britain, Sweden and different parts of North America, cannot be explained without reference to the outcomes of past struggles over the policies of particular organizations and more widespread attempts to win support.

These arguments suggest that *conceptions* of class interests may well be significant elements of political life. They also suggest that class interests as such (that is, as distinct from conceptions of them) perform no explanatory role. In particular, then, the treatment of a variety of distinct agencies, organizations and practices as a social force unified by a common set of class interests has no intellectual foundation.

There is, of course, a sense in which this last point is frequently acknowledged in the literature of class analysis. Exponents of class analysis, marxist and non-marxist alike, write of the need to avoid reductionism. One of the devices they employ is to insist that interests have no existence outside the conditions of their articulation, that they are not sociological givens. Clegg, Boreham and Dow, for example, maintain that the collective interests of a class exist in so far as there are organizations to pursue them. What is at issue then is organizations pursuing objectives relating to their own conceptions of class interests, and possibly pursuing other objectives as well or instead. There is no question here of classes as such operating as social forces. Unfortunately, they continue to write of class struggle and of classes as contending parties in that struggle.

Now, it may seem a little pedantic to insist that classes are not social forces. After all, I argued in chapter 6 that class analysis operates on two distinct levels, with merely a gestural connection between talk of classes and their interests on the one hand and a more or less sophisticated discussion of parties, movements and the like on the other. Perhaps, then, no real harm is done by the reference to classes and their real interests, and it may perform 'an important heuristic function' (Clegg et al., 1986, p. 260). Talk of classes and their interests allows political analysis to bring together a wide range of discrete conditions and struggles into a unified pattern. In the example given at the beginning of this chapter for instance, the development of social policy in the advanced capitalist societies was represented in terms of a struggle between two basic classes and their respective hangers on. The attraction here is that we could discuss social policy and its development without always having to go into the detail of discussion and conflict of the factions, parties and other organizations involved and their often confused and conflicting objectives.

The dangers of that approach have already been indicated. I suggested in chapter 2, for example, that Miliband's appeal in *The State in Capitalist Society* to working class interests that are real but not recognized leads him to pose an entirely imaginary problem, namely, why do the working class (and others) fail to pursue their real interests. A non-existent state of affairs (in which actors do pursue their real interests) is posed as a measure of the present, and the problem is to explain away its non-existence. Miliband has set himself not the task of explaining the decisions that actors take, and the reasons for them, but rather that of accounting for an absence.

For a rather different example, consider Goldthorpe's study of the concomitants of social mobility in Britain. One of Goldthorpe's concerns is overtly political. The working class 'is the social vehicle through whose action' a more open society has by far the best chance of being realized. (1980, p. 28). He therefore studies the implications of social mobility for the conditions of class formation, and in particular for those patterns of 'shared beliefs, attitudes and sentiments that are required for concerted class action' (ibid., p. 265). In effect, he proceeds as if political conclusions regarding the prospects for egalitarian change can be established without reference to the parties, unions and other organizations that are the principal agencies of political struggle in British society or to the forms of calculation in terms of which their struggles are conducted. Once again, the idea of the working class as a social force leads to the posing of an imaginary problem for investigation.

These examples illustrate the general problem with class analysis. The invocation of spurious actors, such as classes, or of their real interests may well serve a polemical purpose – but the practice can hardly be defended on those grounds. Returning finally to the analysis of the development of social policy in contemporary capitalist societies discussed at the beginning of this chapter, it would not be difficult to conclude that Britain's high level of unemployment and its deteriorating social services have come about largely because of the weakness of the working class and the relative strength of its opponents. The problem with this conclusion is not so much that it is wrong, but that it is remarkably uninformative. It strongly suggests that something should be done. Unfortunately, it offers precious little guidance as to *what* should be done to change the complex of parties, unions, employers associations and other organizations at work in our society, the ideologies and forms of political calculation in terms of which they conduct their activities and the patterns of support they enjoy. To the extent that such spurious actors and their supposed interests are called upon to perform an explanatory role, they thoroughly obscure investigation of the conditions in question and political decisions as to what can be done to change them.

Bibliography

For works by Lenin, Marx, Weber etc., dates given in the text are those of the edition used but the date of original publication appears in parentheses in the references below, following the title.

Abercrombie, N. and Urry, J. (1983), *Capital, Labour and the Middle Classes*, London, Allen and Unwin.

Abrams, M., Hinden, R. and Rose, R. (1960), *Must Labour Lose?*, Harmondsworth, Penguin.

Acker, J. (1973), 'Women and Social Stratification: a case of intellectual sexism', *American Journal of Sociology*, 78.

Adlam, D. (1979), 'The case against capitalist patriarchy', *m/f*, 3.

Barrett, M. (1980), *Women's Oppression Today*, London, Verso.

Barrett, M. and McIntosh, M. (1980), 'The "family wage": some problems for feminists and socialists', *Capital and Class*, 11.

Beetham, D. (1974), *Max Weber and the Theory of Modern Politics*, London, Allen and Unwin.

Bernstein, E. (1961), *Evolutionary Socialism*, [1899] New York, Schocken.

Blackburn, R. (ed.) (1972), *Ideology in Social Science*, London, Fontana.

Bottomore, T. B. and Goode, P. (1978), *Austro-Marxism*, Oxford, Clarendon Press.

Braverman, H. (1974), *Labour and Monopoly Capitalism*, New York, Monthly Review Press.

Britten, N. and Heath, A. (1983), 'Women, men and social class', in E. Gamarnikow, D. Morgan, J. Purvis and D. Taylorson (eds), *Gender, Class and Work*, London, Heinemann.

(1984), 'Women's jobs do make a difference', *Sociology*, 18.

Calvert, P. (1982), *The Concept of Class*, London, Hutchinson.

Carchedi, G. (1977), *On the Economic Identification of Social Classes*, London, Routledge and Kegan Paul.

Clegg, S., Boreham, P. and Dow, G. (1986), *Class, Politics and the Economy*, London, Routledge and Kegan Paul.

Cohen, G. A. (1978), *Karl Marx's Theory of History: a defence*, Oxford, Oxford University Press.

Cohen, J. (1983), *Class and Civil Society: the limits of marxian critical theory*, Oxford, Martin Robertson.

Cohen, J. (ed.) (1985), *Social Movements*, winter issue of *Social Research*, 5.

Connolly, W. (1983), *The Terms of Political Discourse*, Oxford, Martin Robertson.

Cottrell, A. (1984), *Social Classes in Marxist Theory*, London, Routledge and Kegan Paul.

Cousins, M. (1978), 'Material arguments and feminism', *m/f*, 2.

Crompton, R. and Gubbay, J. (1977), *Economy and Class Structure*, London, Macmillan.

Crompton, R. and Jones, G. (1984), *White-Collar Proletariat: deskilling and gender in clerical work*, London, Macmillan.

Crosland, C. A. R. (1956), *The Future of Socialism*, London, Cape.

(1960), *Can Labour Win?*, Fabian Tract, 324.

Curtice, J., Heath, A. and Jowell, R. (1985), *How Britain Votes*, Oxford, Pergamon Press.

Cutler, A. J. (1978), 'The romance of labour', *Economy and Society*, 7.

Cutler, A. J., Hindess, B., Hirst, P. Q. and Hussain, A. (1977, 1978), *Marx's Capital and Capitalism Today* (two vols.) London, Routledge and Kegan Paul.

(1979), 'An imaginary orthodoxy', *Economy and Society*, 8.

Dahrendorf, R. (1959), *Class and Class Conflict in Industrial Society*, London, Routledge and Kegan Paul.

(1969), 'The service class', in T. Burns (ed.), *Industrial Man*, Harmondsworth, Penguin.

Delphy, C. (1984), *Close to Home*, London, Hutchinson.

Esping-Anderson, G. (1985), *Politics against Markets: the social-democratic road to power*, Princeton, Princeton University Press.

Esping-Anderson, G. and Korpi, W. (1984), 'Social Policy as Class Politics in Post-War Capitalism', in J. H. Goldthorpe (ed.) (1984).

Firestone, S. (1972), *The Dialectic of Sex*, New York, Bantam.

Franklin, M. (1985), *The Decline of Class Voting in Britain*, Oxford, Oxford University Press.

Furbank, P. N. (1985), *Unholy Pleasure or the Idea of Social Class*, Oxford, Oxford University Press.

Garnsey, E. (1978), 'Women's Work and Theories of Class Stratification', *Sociology*, 12.

Giddens, A. (1973), *The Class Structure of the Advanced Societies*, London, Hutchinson.

Goldthorpe, J. H. (1980), *Social Mobility and Class Structure in Modern Britain*, Oxford, Clarendon Press.

(1983), 'Women and Class Analysis: in defence of the conventional view', *Sociology*, 17.

(1984a), 'Introduction' in J. H. Goldthorpe (ed.) (1984).

(1984b), 'The end of convergence: corporatist and dualist tendencies in modern western societies', in J. H. Goldthorpe (ed.) (1984).

(1984c), 'Women and class analysis: a reply to the critics', *Sociology*, 18.

Goldthorpe, J. H. (ed.) (1984), *Order and Conflict in Contemporary Capitalism*, Oxford, Clarendon Press.

Goldthorpe, J. H. and Lockwood, D. (1963), 'Affluence and the British class structure', *Sociological Review*, 11.

Goldthorpe, J. H., Lockwood, D., Bechofer, F. and Platt, J. (1968), *The Affluent Worker*, Cambridge, Cambridge University Press.

Hall, S. (1978), 'The "political" and the "economic" in Marx's theory of classes', in A. Hunt (ed.), *Class and Class Structure*, London, Lawrence and Wishart.

Harris, L. (1978), 'The Science of the Economy', *Economy and Society*, 7.

Heath, A. (1981), *Social Mobility*, London, Fontana.

Hindess, B. (1977), *Philosophy and Methodology in the Social Sciences*, Brighton, Harvester.

(1982), 'The politics of social mobility', *Economy and Society*, 11.

(1983), *Parliamentary Democracy and Socialist Politics*, London, Routledge and Kegan Paul.

(1984), 'Rational choice theory and the analysis of political action', *Economy and Society*, 13.

(1986a), 'Actors and social relations', in M. Wardell and S. Turner (eds.), *Sociological Theory in Transition*, London, Allen and Unwin.

(1986b), 'Interests in Political Analysis', in J. Law (ed.), *Power, Action and Belief*, Sociological Review Monograph, 32, London, Routledge and Kegan Paul.

Hobsbawm, E. (1983), 'Labour's lost millions', *Marxism Today*, September 1983.

(1984), 'Labour: rump or rebirth', *Marxism Today*, March 1984.

(1985), 'The retreat into extremism', *Marxism Today*, April 1985.

Humphries, J. (1977), 'Class struggle and the persistence of the working class family', *Cambridge Journal of Economics*, 1.

James, S. (1984), *The Content of Social Explanation*, Cambridge, Cambridge University Press.

Johnston, L. (1986), *Marxism, Class Analysis and Socialist Pluralism*, London, Allen and Unwin.

Kautsky, K. (1964), *The Dictatorship of the Proletariat*, [1918] Ann Arbor, University of Michigan Press.

(1971), *The Class Struggle*, New York, W. W. Norton.

Korpi, W. (1983), *The Democratic Class Struggle*, London, Routledge and Kegan Paul.

Lenin, V. I. (1964a), *The State and Revolution*, [1917] *Collected Works*, 25, London, Lawrence and Wishart.

(1964b), *The Proletarian Revolution and the Renegade Kautsky*, [1918] *Collected Works*, vol. 28, London, Lawrence and Wishart.

(1964c), 'The discussion of self-determination summed up', [1916] *Collected Works*, 22, London, Lawrence and Wishart .

Lévi-Strauss, C. (1966), *The Savage Mind*, London, Weidenfeld and Nicolson.

(1969), *The Elementary Structures of Kinship*, London, Eyre and Spottiswood.

Lockwood, D. (1958), *The Blackcoated Worker*, London, Allen and Unwin.

Marx, K. (1966), *Capital*, 3, [1894] London, Lawrence and Wishart.

(1968), 'The Eighteenth Brumaire of Louis Bonaparte', [1852] in Marx and Engels, *Selected Works*, London, Lawrence and Wishart.

(1969), *Theories of Surplus Value*, [1905–1910] London, Lawrence and Wishart.

(1971), *A Contribution to the Critique of Political Economy*, London, [1859] Lawrence and Wishart.

Marx, K. and Engels, F. (1968), *The Communist Manifesto*, [1848] in Marx and Engels, *Selected Works*, London, Lawrence and Wishart.

(1976). *The German Ideology*, Moscow, Progress Publishers.

(n.d.), *Selected Correspondence*, Moscow, Foreign Languages Publishing House.

Miliband, R. (1969), *The State in Capitalist Society*, London, Weidenfeld and Nicolson.

(1972), 'The capitalist state', in Blackburn (ed.) (1972).

Mommsen, W. (1974), *The Age of Bureaucracy*, Oxford, Blackwell.

Panitch, L. (1986), *Working Class Politics in Crisis*, London, Verso.

Parkin, F. (1979), *Marxism and Class Theory: a bourgeois critique*, London, Tavistock.

Poulantzas, N. (1972), 'The problem of the capitalist state', in R. Blackburn (ed.) (1972).

——— (1975), *Classes in Contemporary Capitalism*, London, New Left Books .

Przeworski, A. (1977), 'From proletariat into Class: the process of class formation from Kautsky's *The Class Struggle* to recent debates', *Politics and Society*, 7.

Renner, K. (1978), 'The service class', English translation [1953] in T. B. Bottomore and P. Goode (1978).

Roberts, K., Cook, F. G., Clark, S. C. and Semeonoff, E. (1977), *The Fragmentary Class Structure*, London, Heinemann.

Robertson, D. (1984), *Class and the British Electorate*, Oxford, Blackwell.

Roemer, J. (1982), *A General Theory of Exploitation and Class*, Cambridge, Mass., Harvard University Press.

Rose, R. and McAllister, I. (1986), *Voters Begin to Choose*, London, Sage.

Scott, J. (1982), *The Upper Classes*, London, Macmillan.

Stanworth, M. (1984), 'Women and Class Analysis: a reply to Goldthorpe', *Sociology*, 18.

Steedman, I. (ed.) (1981), *The Value Controversy*, London, Verso.

Stephens, J. D. (1979), *The Transition from Capitalism to Socialism*, London, Macmillan.

Therborn, G. (1986), *Why Are Some Peoples More Unemployed Than Others?*, London, Verso.

Weber, M. (1968), *Economy and Society*, [1922] New York, Bedminster Press.

——— (1978), 'Class, status groups and parties', [1922], in *Max Weber: Selections in Translation* (ed. Runciman), Cambridge, Cambridge University Press.

Wilensky, H. (1975), *The Welfare State and Equality*, Berkeley, University of California Press.

Wilson, E. O. (1975), *Sociobiology: the new synthesis*, Cambridge, Mass., Harvard University Press.

——— (1978), *On Human Nature*, Cambridge, Mass., Harvard University Press.

Wright, E. O. (1978), *Class, Crisis and the State*, London, New Left Books.

——— (1980), 'Varieties of marxist conceptions of class structure', *Politics and Society*, 9.

——— (1985), *Classes*, London, Verso.

Index

Coventry University